the rock cycle

River Teeth Literary Nonfiction Prize
Daniel Lehman and Joe Mackall, SERIES EDITORS

The River Teeth Literary Nonfiction Prize is awarded to the best work of literary nonfiction submitted to the annual contest sponsored by *River Teeth: A Journal of Nonfiction Narrative.*

Also available in the River Teeth Literary Nonfiction Prize series:

Try to Get Lost: Essays by Joan Frank
I Am a Stranger Here Myself by Debra Gwartney
MINE: Essays by Sarah Viren
Rough Crossing: An Alaskan Fisherwoman's Memoir by Rosemary McGuire
The Girls in My Town: Essays by Angela Morales

the rock cycle

essays

Kevin Honold

University of New Mexico Press | Albuquerque

Printed in the United States of America

978-0-8263-6243-8 (paper)
978-0-8263-6244-5 (e-book)

Library of Congress Control Number: 2020949842

Cover illustration adapted from photograph by Kunj Parekh on Unsplash
Designed by Felicia Cedillos
Composed in Adobe Garamond Pro 10.25/14.25

We wait for light, but it is darkness; for brightness,
but we walk in darkness.
—*Isaiah*

For there is a dim glimmering of light yet un-put-out, in men:
let them walk, let them walk, that the darkness overtake them not.
—*Augustine*

contents

acknowledgments

The author is grateful to the following publications, in which some of these essays previously appeared in slightly different form.

Antioch Review: "Light Discipline"
Border Crossing: "Winter in the Capital" (published as "Wordsworth in Mongolia")
Fourth Genre: "Spring Arrives in the Gobi"
Hudson Review: "A Brief History of the Huron" (forthcoming) and "Verdun"
Image: "The Cloud of Unknowing"
The Louisville Review: "King Oedipus"
River Teeth: "Cycling the Mojave"

King Oedipus

Arabian Desert, 1991

One night we got lost. Running low on fuel, uncertain of our location respective of the border, far from base, we came across a Bedouin camp in the dark. Two men with Kalashnikovs emerged from a tent. Lieutenant Gerstenberger, twenty-three years old, recent graduate of West Point, stepped forward and asked the men if they knew of other soldiers in the vicinity, namely, soldiers dressed like himself. By way of demonstration, he helpfully tugged at the sleeve of his uniform and gestured over his shoulder at us, toward five figures in forest camouflage standing at the edge of the light. The nomads muttered among themselves. One man shook his head and repeated, over and over, a word we didn't understand. The tone, however, was plain enough, so we returned to our vehicles and drove off. The lieutenant was a decent man. He wasn't looking to make trouble. I wonder where he is these days.

South Texas, January, 2007

At the midpoint of the bridge over the Nueces River, I lean the bike against the guardrail and look for signs of life in the stony channel. A procession of half and quarter moons of still water reflects blue sky as the clouds begin to disperse, and my shadow is a welcome apparition after several days of rain. In the thorny scrub along the river, the white tail of a deer flits twice and disappears.

Two zone-tailed hawks cruise the low brown hills. The four-foot wingspans and silent circling flight are believed by ornithologists to deceive smaller birds, who mistake the hawks for nonpredatory turkey vultures. The birds' shadows race across the riverbed.

A cloud passes over the sun, the land fades, and the pools of blue water turn gray. I pedal the remaining forty miles into a cold wind, to the town of Bracketville.

Nothing in Bracketville is so useless it can be thrown out. Gas cans, tires worn to the cables, kitchen chairs, and aluminum doors accumulate behind sheds, along fences. Boat paddles, tricycles, camouflage coveralls. Paint pots. Ladder jacks, strollers, PVC pipe, a crutch without a mate. A coil of gray wire hangs like a wreath on a garage wall.

Attached to the town's lone gas station is a kitchen that serves burritos and corn dogs. There are tables along the window where I sit and warm my hands on a paper cup of coffee, mulling over money and weather, watching the truck traffic shuttle past on US 90, feeling thoroughly discouraged. An old man in a cowboy hat dozes on a bench. He surfaces once to mumble at the patrons, then slips back into sleep. It's a long way to California.

Outside of town, I stick out a thumb. The Border Patrol truck rolls up beside me. Banners of mud are pasted to the truck's quarter panels. Through the passenger window, the young agent asks questions about my bike, my destination. "Someone called us about some guy taking his clothes off in a ditch back there," he says, glancing back toward Uvalde.

"That was probably me, officer," I tell him. "I was putting my long underwear on."

Something doesn't seem right, but he decides I'm Anglo enough and pulls away.

I stick out a thumb again. A pickup passes, doubles back. The woman and child have already climbed into the back seat of the cab as the man pulls alongside.

"I saw this guy standing on the road," he says through the passenger window, “and I thought, man, he looks cold! I better give him a ride.” He helps me lift the bike into the truck’s bed.

The woman wears wire-rimmed glasses and her black hair tied with a rubber band at the back of her neck. She and the boy lean forward, shoulder to shoulder, between and behind the man and me. They are taking the boy to a doctor in Del Rio. “He fell off a ladder,” she says. The boy is to have pins inserted in his left elbow, which was fractured in two places. The man, Paul, talks about winter weather that won’t move off, and the football playoffs. And tarantulas, because I asked. He’s a Steelers fan. He works for the railroad. “I like it. It’s hard sometimes, you know?”

We arrive at Del Rio and he helps me unload the bike and shakes my hand. “No more falling off ladders,” I say to the boy, and I thank the woman, both of whose names I’ve neglected to ask.

3

Highway 90 in Del Rio is a five-lane boulevard lined with body shops, fast-food places, motels. Ice and snow hit the town over the preceding days, and the city has spread a sand mix on the streets. Today the streets are fairly dry, and cars and trucks plow through the roiling dust like wagons through a high-plains town. A brief spell of sunshine and a warm breeze are enough to dry my damp clothes. The dust has a salt taste and I spit as I pedal, looking for a cheap room, singing along to some song in my head.

Grackles and crows are common in the neighborhoods behind the strip malls that line US 90. Town birds: clever, alternately biding and raucous, instinctively opportunistic. The crow, it’s said, is the only one of God’s creatures that’s smarter than it needs to be. “Crows are black all over the world”: that’s a Chinese proverb, and it suits many occasions.

The Del Rio grackles operate in ill-disciplined bands, in parking lots, in back lots, in gutters. The guide describes their voice as “a rising screech, like a rusty hinge,” but a hinge is mechanical, predictable, passive. The grackle’s voice startles; it’s loud, sudden, tropical. Fruitier than a hinge, its song contains the slightest electronic burr, like interference from a rogue satellite. When perched and alone, the grackle cries out as though it periodically astonishes itself. But in society it behaves differently, like many people we know. When foraging with its cousins, I've noticed, it's workmanlike and it does not talk.

A quiet afternoon. Cats prowl and pause to listen. The pavement is poorly patched. Cakes of asphalt rise like basaltic atolls from street-wide puddles of snowmelt. The glue scent of stripping agent drifts from the open bays of a body shop.

US 90 declines gradually to the south, then doglegs east, but if you continue straight at the bend, across the overpass that spans the railroad tracks, you come to the old town of Del Rio. Looking down from the overpass, one sees empty quart bottles and trash, a sodden heap of clothes, a laceless red shoe. An expired shopping cart lies in a puddle between empty tracks that lead off to water towers, transmission derricks, brown sky, Mexico.

I decide, after some debate, against sleeping outdoors. The thought of another damp and freezing night in the bivouac tent is hateful. The decision brings relief bordering on elation. The reasoning faculty is a keen litigator on behalf of every weakness. Indulgent, reliably inconsistent, it labors for my well-being day and night, for free.

I check into a room at the Cielito Lindo. Pretty little heaven? Pretty little sky?

The three women who run the used-clothing store trade jokes across racks of dresses and winter jackets. They place their hands on one another's shoulders as they sidle past each other in the narrow aisles. When I make my way to the register with two pairs of socks, they gather at the counter for a chat about the weather. One of them asks if I have a winter jacket. A homeless shelter is two doors down. Probably, she thinks I'm staying there.

"I got arthritis, diabetes, and three screws in my knee," the woman at the register says, by way of commiseration or, perhaps, by way of gently preempting any undue shame on my part.

"Rosie," she calls out, "you got any quarters?"

She shows me the tag stapled to the sock. "Honey, what's that number there? This old dog can't see like she once did." When I tell her, she presses numbers, one by one, on the register. A look of happy surprise crosses her face when the cash drawer slides open.

"Well! That's twenty-six cents." She gives me the change. "You stay warm out there, baby."

It's quiet in the old town, a cold wet morning. I pause on the empty sidewalk. A buzzy sound I've never heard is a brown-crested flycatcher, umber and olive with a five-inch tail, perched on a telephone pole.

I've brought with me a volume of Greek tragedies. Of Oedipus's children, his two daughters—Antigone and Ismene—remained his "staff and his support" through his long homelessness, while his sons fell to killing one another for the remains of the kingdom. Oedipus was fated by "an unspeakable star" to wander the thirsty places of the earth. Everywhere he went, rumor of his crimes preceded him, and people closed their hearts to him, because men do shut their doors against a setting sun. Only when he came to Colonus, and was greeted there by Theseus, King of Athens, did Oedipus find solace and a kind word. Gentle Theseus, who had known his own hard roads.

> Tell me. It would be something dire indeed
> To make me leave you comfortless; for I
> Too was an exile. I grew up abroad,
> And in strange lands have fought as few men have
> With danger and with death.
> Therefore no wanderer shall come, as you do,
> And be denied my audience or aid.
> I know I am only a man; I have no more
> To hope for in the end than you have.[1]

The entire world is Oedipus's place of exile, with few landmarks to navigate by. The world to him is a desert. He has only the touch of his daughters' hands to bind him to the earth.

Rain falls periodically, cold and steady. The weather aggravates the tendons in my knees. That's what I tell myself as I pay for another night. In truth I enjoy my tidy little room at the Cielito Lindo, watching the Weather Channel, drinking Carlo Rossi, rereading old plays I'd read before but never quite understood, and still don't. I'm down to a few hundred dollars and the room is $35 a night. I have to get outside again, but I can't bring myself to do it. I find it easy to talk myself out of riding. It's raining; my knees hurt; the snow in the Pecos River valley is heading this way. I wake up and open the door and find it's still raining, and the decision makes itself. Then I buy a couple forties of Old Milwaukee and open a book. Here's the chorus in *Alcestis*:

> I myself, in the transports
> of mystic verses, as in study
> of history and science, have found
> nothing so strong as Compulsion
> nor any means to combat her,
> not in the Thracian books set down
> in verse by the school of Orpheus,
> not in all the remedies Phoebus has given the heirs
> of Asclepius to fight the many afflictions of man.[2]

Sooner or later I will have to get on the bike; it's a long way to the Mojave. Weather cannot be helped, and money will run out. On the television that evening, the president gives a speech about the war. It is to be escalated.

The Bacchae is a strange tale. The unbeliever as well as the believer are horribly punished, and I find that confusing. When the sober and imperious young ruler Pentheus is informed that the women of the kingdom, including his own mother, are debauched in the forest meadows—decked in bryony, crowned with laurels of ivy and oak, suckling wolf cubs in their calmer moments, running with the wild animals and drunk on wine—he determines to lead his soldiers out to quell the mischief. But Dionysus, in whose honor the revels go on, appears to Pentheus disguised in the mask of a beautiful smiling young man, and casts a spell on him.

Enchanted by the god, Pentheus agrees to go alone and unprotected, accompanied only by the eastern stranger. He is persuaded to disguise himself as a woman to avoid detection. In a narcotic transport, Pentheus delights in his new faun-dappled robe and in his new golden tresses, and he gladly allows the god to preen him in preparation. In the woods, Pentheus is discovered and, in a frenzy, the women mistake him for a lion and tear him to pieces with their nails and teeth. His mother carries Pentheus's head triumphantly into town, stroking the soft down of her son's cheek as though it were a lion's mane.

Arabian Desert, 1991

We sit on our packs beside our vehicles, waiting to cross the border from Saudi Arabia to Iraq. Blue skies, cool and quiet, no birds that I can remember. Some soldiers write letters. The desert at noon has the stillness of the day after the last day of the world. The low rise we occupy slips away at every point to the immense horizon, and the sky seals the land like a rinsed jar.

Mark from Reno has been irritable lately. His German girlfriend is pregnant and she refuses to get an abortion, according to her last letter. Now he sets out a small battery-powered tape deck and plays the Doors' "The End." Somebody complains about the choice, to no avail.

Tom and I walk off and find an abandoned Bedouin camp, empty milk bottles scattered about a scorched circle in the sand. We take turns tossing the bottles high in the air and throwing rocks at them, like skeet shooters. A bottle bursts and the shards fall in a belled shower of spangling rainbow light.

Someone shouts for us, and we drop the rocks and the bottles. It's time to load up, and we form a column in front of the berm—the sand wall—that serves as the international border. Rocket rounds, bright as flares, arc overhead. Engineers blow a gap in the wall and we drive through. An army photographer, standing on the berm, records the event with a video camera.

Resistance was brushed aside during the first day and a half. Men in filthy uniforms emerged from their bunkers with their hands held out, more in supplication than in surrender, but we didn't stop for them. Their faces were creased from the strain of weeks of bombardment. On the second and third days, however, retreating Iraqi forces managed on a few occasions to set up defensive positions, and the advance stuttered. While fighter bombers and helicopters pounded the Iraqi vehicles to our front, we climbed out of our vehicles, lay down in the sand, and watched.

The incandescent shells from American tanks sailed, unerring as arrows, toward enemy armor a kilometer and more away. Pillars of smoke rose like black beanstalks from the desert floor. In the distance, groups of men ran in different directions, and I could not say where they were headed. The act of running struck me as an absurd and useless activity on a battlefield that afforded nothing in the way of cover. Those men merely wanted to get away—somewhere, anywhere—but they were not going to outrun Bradley Fighting Vehicles and M1A1 tanks that burned two gallons of fuel per mile. And if the tankers missed them, the prowling helicopters would not. Those who managed to evade capture or death by day would turn up later, after the sun went down, as luminescent specters on night-vision viewfinders.

After these brief actions, we climbed back into our vehicles and I drove, weaving around the CBUs, or cluster bomb units, the bread loaf–sized bomblets dropped by US aircraft. Many of them lay scattered about, unexploded, and the man seated beside me shouted again and again to *pay attention, goddamnit.* Watch it. There's one, see it? There's one. *There.*

We picked our way forward in this manner, by fits and starts, following the tanks. Word spread that mines had damaged some vehicles and injured some people, but I didn't see it. By then the sky had turned overcast.

In the vehicle with me were two others. Robert Haviland was from the Florida panhandle. The son of poor missionaries, he had spent his childhood in impoverished African villages. And Mike Sweeney from Knoxville, who sat quietly in the back seat and looked out the window and did not speak unless spoken to. Haviland was a good soldier and was unimpressed by Mike and me. I suspect that, more than anything, he loved the army because for the first time in his life he got three square meals a day and disposable cash.

Mike did nothing except under threat of punitive action, and for this reason we called him Sloth. He had no friends that I knew of, but didn't seem the worse for that. Aloof, untrimmed, and rumpled, he had a broad Irish face and a tired smile, as if he'd just woken up, as though he'd accidentally wandered into your dream, or you into his. He kept his nose in a sci-fi novel whenever he was not under direct orders to be otherwise occupied, and he inhabited a different world, one I imagine was possessed of magic stones and forbidding islands.

I wonder where Mike is now. I wonder what he was thinking, staring out at the desert, sitting so quietly behind me I often forgot he was there. I bet he doesn't think much about it. He was one of those people for whom this thing we call "the real world" is just so much pretense and make-believe, remarkable only in its absurdity. Long after I left the army, I struggled through a book that sought to explain Hegel's Idealism, in which both the real and the rational are comprehended in something the philosopher called the Absolute. This Absolute, Hegel said, is essentially spiritual and may be called, among other things, God; for this reason, God is a sort of process in which the individual mind actively participates. I'm still not certain in what sense, or to what degree, such things as blind kings, flycatchers, or CBUs participate in this Absolute. If I knew where Mike Sweeney was, I would write to him and ask his opinion. I'm confident that his response would be thoughtful and sincere. You can't trust just anybody with questions like that.

For twenty-five years, not a day has gone by when I haven't remembered those months. Small things will call me back: the smell of sun-warmed canvas, the smell of instant coffee. The wheezy, rattly sound of diesel engines. Sand, generally. If I see a black beetle, it is March 1991 once more. Teenagers in unlaced combat boots annoy me to an unreasonable degree. Recollections are neither welcome nor unwelcome because they seem to have involved a different person. More and more, those memories play out in a different order of time: increasingly vivid, increasingly remote. I bet Mike doesn't think about it for months at a time. Years, maybe. The whole miserable thing may have, by now, entirely slipped from his mind.

The heaviest action occurred on the third day of the ground fighting when our unit, Second Armored Cavalry Regiment, met a brigade of retreating Republican Guard from the Hammurabi Division, which had turned about to face us. Drifting smoke and rain, by a trick of vision, narrowed the distances between things. Vehicles sped in different directions, near and far away, or stood fast and burned. Men ran without weapons, helicopter gunships swept the field. In short order, the regiment's M1s and Bradleys destroyed a few hundred Iraqi vehicles, killed hundreds of crewmen, and left a desert pillared with columns of smoke. That night, the company circled in Conestoga fashion. Outside our charmed ring of vehicles, the regimental tanks prowled, dispatching survivors. Vehicles burned in the dark like so many blazing haystacks. I woke from a doze to see a damaged Iraqi personnel carrier moving toward us from a hundred meters off. A white round from an M1 hit it broadside. The carrier rolled on a short distance, began to smoke, and no one climbed out.

US casualties were light. In military records it was named the Battle of 73 Easting, after the coordinate location, there being no nearby town or geographical feature with which to label the thing: no Stone Mountain, no Brandywine Creek. It was neither consequential nor much remembered.

A few nights later, drawn by a strange glow in the southern sky, we climbed a high dune and found the horizon on fire. Retreating Iraqi forces had blown the Kuwaiti oil wells. Tom and I sat on the crest of the dune with an Egyptian soldier and a Kuwaiti interpreter. These two had fallen in with us somehow, somewhere along the way. The interpreter buried his face in his hands and wept. I was mesmerized by that wall of flames, as one confronted for the first time with mountains draped in ice, or a storm coming in from the sea.

That fire still watches me. Some years ago, I came across these words by the fourteenth-century Fleming, Jan van Ruysbroeck: "What we are, that we gaze at; and what we gaze at, that we are."[3] That made a good deal of sense. Five hundred years after Ruysbroeck, Gerard Manley Hopkins wrote that "what you look hard at seems to look hard at you." I wonder if Hopkins read Ruysbroeck.

Another five hundred years, I suppose, will pass before this awful secret once again occurs to some thoughtful soul, a man or woman seated alone at a window, watching the sun set over a desert. Wickedness is the one irreducible fact, so obvious it sometimes eludes me, like the essential flaw in a person's character that is visible to everyone but him.

I sometimes wish I were back on that dune that night. I imagine putting my hand on the Kuwaiti's shoulder and saying, "That's some tough shit, buddy. Guess you'll have to get a fucking job now." No doubt, he got his oil money back.

For a week following that night, we moved under a stratum of ash that sat a hundred feet off the ground. The ash turned the sun into a bleary puddle, filtering its light into a submarine green, like the light at the bottom of a pool. Vehicles and people stood forth in a strange and shadowless clarity.

I was a radio jammer, but we never did jam enemy communications, and only a few times during the ground operation did we even set up the transmitter. I felt like a spectator more than a participant, like a civilian on a police ride-along. It was the tankers' show; the desert was ideal for mechanized operations. Electronic countermeasures like radio jamming were simply not as effective as uranium-tipped, armor-piercing shells. In the end, many Iraqi formations slipped out of the US Army's encircling movement. These units reappeared weeks later to crush Kurdish and Shiite uprisings with ferocious efficiency.

After the cease-fire was announced, Sergeant Haviland and Tom and others spent time driving around the battlefield, plotting the coordinates of Iraqi corpses, that they might be buried by Graves Registration units. I did not participate. I declined to be involved at that point. I sat in the tent or in the vehicle and read through the Hermann Hesse novels I'd dug up from the bottom of my duffel bag. I talked to no one, and I refused to look.

Only one opportunity to be useful presented itself to me during the deployment to the Persian Gulf, and I rejected it. For that moral dereliction, for declining to join in my fellow soldiers' efforts to bring some measure of dignity to those who had been killed, I will always be sorry. There must be few things more shameful than to be held cheap by the dead.

We drove on and relieved the airborne and air assault units that had leapfrogged the armored columns and seized the Tigris and Euphrates bridges. I remember driving in column down a highway littered with twisted metal and broken asphalt, in the weird green light, through a lifeless landscape riven by erosion and wadis. I cannot recall seeing trees or buildings in that place. By then, the oil smoke had spilled to every corner of the sky and the sun gleamed dully at midday like a coin in a fountain.

As the highway dipped toward the Euphrates, the roadside cutbanks rose at either hand and gradually hemmed us in. The soldiers we had come to relieve had dug holes into these banks, and now they emerged from their caves in filthy and variously configured uniforms. In my memory, they evinced neither gladness nor even recognition of us, but merely stood in their mismatched uniforms and watched as we passed, and I don't recall if we stopped or if we acknowledged them. Nor do I recall where we were headed as we crossed the bridge and entered the open desert again. From this point and extending several days, perhaps a week or two, my memory is blank.

Largely and probably rightly forgotten (a friend calls it "that thing in the Gulf"), it was a brief conflict noteworthy mainly for the subsequent failure among political leaders to draw useful conclusions. The United States was experiencing a painful recession in 1991, and the short and successful war was not long on peoples' minds. The swiftness of destruction, the demonstration of devastating military power, seemed to herald something new in warfare, but events would soon put that notion to rest.

After we deployed back to Germany, a ceremony took place on the barracks' parade ground. Left to right in front of our assembled ranks, five riderless black horses were led in file. In keeping with cavalry practice going back to the days of the Indian wars, empty black boots were placed backward in the stirrups for the five soldiers from the regiment who had been killed. I did not know any of those five men, but I sometimes think about the combined span of those unlived years, and I wonder whether what I have done with my life is sufficient. *Sufficient* is not the right word, but I cannot come up with a better one, and maybe there isn't one after all. I sometimes feel that I have not honored them—not the Americans, not the Iraqis, not any of the tens of thousands of dead. Only one thing is beyond doubt: too much time has been wasted.

Some days after the ceremony on the parade ground, on a Sunday afternoon, Tom and I sat in the barracks watching the victory parade in New York City on Armed Forces TV. All those guys in pressed desert fatigues marching flawlessly without weapons down Fifth Avenue . . . Who were they? What were they doing? We made jokes, embarrassed somehow, for many reasons. At the time, I could not have spelled it out, and I still don't know how. I am afraid to get things wrong.

I won't speak for Tom. He was the only person from my unit I kept in touch with—for a few years anyway, until we drifted out of contact. He was often working on, and never quite finishing, a play about himself and his ex-wife called *The Prince and the Tramp*. Last I knew, he was employed as a mechanic for the Wichita Police Department. A smart guy, a good friend. I hope he's found a peaceful life. I hope he's finished the play.

The Army was downsizing rapidly in late 1991. Every day, planes filled with GIs departed Germany, bound for Fort Dix, New Jersey, to be discharged. There, we attended a class on how to file for unemployment benefits, then we were issued air tickets home. The dishonorably discharged were issued bus tickets.

I wish, instead of a class on jobless benefits, we'd been given forty hours of community service, in nursing homes or VA medical centers. Not as busywork, but as means to refocus, to reorient, something to take us out of ourselves to a place where young men do their best. Looking back, I wish we had been brought to the local library and told to write ten-page essays on the role of augury in Sumerian religious ceremony, or something like that. Of course, these would have been hateful ideas, and I would have enthusiastically joined the rest in damning the silly ass that thought them up.

We arrived late at the terminal for the evening's last round of departures, and soldiers sprinted for the gates like they were running for their lives. Several of us missed our flights. We sprawled on the padded chairs and talked. You get used to waiting.

In the room at Cielito Lindo, I finish reading the story of the blind, lost king. The chorus at Colonus passes judgment on an old man who is seeking a death that is not dishonorable. It's a funny thing about the chorus. They can be pretty obtuse at times.

Though he has watched a decent age pass by,
A man will sometimes still desire the world.
I swear I see no wisdom in that man.[4]

Oedipus, forgive me. I know that I, too, would have denied you. I'm a slave, just like the rest of them.

According to the forecaster on the television, the Rio Grande valley is under a low pressure system. We can expect clouds and snow to linger into next week, she says.

I pull a chair to the window. Snow gusts in the streetlights on Highway 90.

Light Discipline

Texas, March

Water is transient in the Big Bend of the Rio Grande, but my map indicated scattered springs, each within a day's hike of the next. A snowstorm had blanketed the region a month before, so I was reasonably hopeful to find water running at those springs.

Small cairns marked the trail where it was crosscut by arroyos. The silence was broken only by ravens and the scuff of my shoes on black rock and sand. Shadows dissolved as the sun climbed, the desert unfolded in stark lines, and when I stopped to listen, silence gathered like an element. People speak of silence "falling," but in truth it rises from the ground, like mist.

In the evening I came to the Rio Grande and set up my tent under a stand of flood-twisted tamarisks. On the gravel bank, I boiled water for oatmeal and coffee as the sun set over Mariscal Mountain, a long ridge running to 3,900 feet. Across the river, hidden by trees, a few cows browsed. The listless jangle of bells and the workaday Spanish of the ranch hands carried clearly over the water. When the men and animals moved on, only the sound of water flowing through the reeds remained.

The bell of the sky smoldered at the horizon that evening, and the moon rose bright as horn, while the sun, dust-dimmed, set in a blood-in-water haze. Like equal weights in the pans of a scale, the sun and moon held the beam of the desert, for a moment, in balance. Then the sky tipped, the spell broke, and the first star appeared.

The mountains and sky conspired to fill me with an overwhelming sense of gratitude. It's strange, this gratefulness for the givenness of things. The beauty of desert mountains, or of any lovely place, is a gift I have done nothing to deserve, and therefore can never requite. It's at that point that gratitude distills into something like despair, and there's nothing to do but sit and watch.

Solitude is welcome but wearying company. The heightened awareness of being alone is a low-watt point of warmth at the back of the neck. If desert solitude is unsettling, it is not due to fear, I think, but to the intimation or suspicion of something that has come and gone.

Solitude lends a fugitive quality to deserts. Even if I stand on high ground, with a view of scores of square miles, and I take in whole ranges of mountains at a glance, the desert's center is forever beyond the next ridge, just out of sight, right over there. At noon, the desert's center corresponds to the subsolar point, but only for an hour.

Thousands of holy men and women disappeared into the deserts of Syria and Egypt in the third and fourth centuries. Many of them were from Europe's most educated and privileged classes, like Saint Anthony who, after the death of his parents, put his young sister in a convent, gave away his inheritance, and boarded ship. In the caves outside of the Egyptian town of Oxyrhynchus, at the beginning of the fourth century, there were reported to be as many as thirty thousand religious, seekers, and pilgrims, and it is said that women outnumbered men there. Even if the careless math of that age is accounted for, the numbers are remarkable.

They fled a spiritual desert for a true one and came face to face with themselves. Many broke under the strain of exposure and deprivation. Others, hoping to commune with God, found instead hunger, sickness, wild animals, poisonous snakes, and thirst. I wonder why there is not a similar movement today. There can be little doubt that the threats facing us, though different in kind, are at least as grave as those faced by the West during the decline of the empire.

In the desert, notions of order and disorder are irrelevant. All learned systems of comparative values, all codes by which one navigates society and steers clear of prison or opprobrium, all modes of understanding, become, after a time, impertinent. Maybe that's why those men and women went to the caves.

Barry Lopez, in *Crossing Open Ground*, touches on this otherness. He is writing here of a hike to the floor of the Grand Canyon:

> It is this known dimension of distance and time and the perplexing question posed by the canyon itself—What is consequential? (in one's life, in the life of human beings, in the life of a planet)—that reverberate constantly, and make the human inclination to judge (another person, another kind of thought) seem so eerie.

Maybe I love this world too much to leave it, to bid farewell to city, to family, to everything I know, to go to live in a lonely place, there to pray for the healing of man's despair and for an end to his self-hatred.

Or, what's more likely, I don't love this world enough.

There's a curious story in Benedicta Ward's translation of *The Desert Fathers*:

> Macarius the Great said to the brothers in Scetis after a service in church, "Flee, my brothers." One of the brothers said to him, "Abba, where can we flee when we are already in the desert?" He put his finger upon his lips and said: "I tell you, you must flee this." Then he went into his cell, shut the door, and remained alone.[1]

A person is said to be "beside himself" when experiencing extreme joy or rage. The phrase appears in the book of Acts, when Paul testifies before King Agrippa, confessing how he had persecuted innocent people and had been struck by a strange light. And now, he tells the King, the dead have come to life, which is no cause for wonder, since the prophets had foretold it. At this point the procurator of Judea, named Porcius Festus, interrupts the old man, who is clearly unwell, and says, "Paul! Thou art beside thyself. Much learning doth make thee mad."[2]

Beside oneself.

It's interesting how feelings of fury or ecstasy visit us like half-forgotten companions, more or less welcome.

The desert, too, is a kind of visitation. When I recollect that I'm alone, it's then that I have company. Solitude, like a shadow, has a way of walking beside you. Marco Polo wrote about the Gobi djinns that called out to passing merchants, who followed the voices into the desert, lost their ways, and were never seen again.

More than once during this hike I've sat alone and watched the darkness gather and wanted nothing more than to get far, far away.

Dammam, Saudi Arabia, 1990

In the morning at the staging area, thousands of soldiers—British, Egyptian, American, Saudi—lined up in differently shaded, green uniforms for powdered eggs and syrupy peach slices. They stood in a meandering line that stretched back far into the desert, and it seemed as if a grand endeavor were underway, the significance of which was not entirely clear to me. I did not feel like a soldier, but an uninvited observer, a visitor of small consequence. What could all this possibly have to do with me? Perhaps it was the subdued talk of all those men, something secretive and guarded in their demeanor. The Arab soldiers comported themselves with a kind of standoffish fatalism, as though they had seen all this before. Everyone just seemed to *know*.

Dave Kavanagh, a member of my platoon, had been a high school English teacher before enlisting. He was a Czech linguist, a radio interceptor. He and the other Czech linguists in my unit went to Prague once, after the Gulf deployment, as part of a diplomatic mission. The Berlin Wall and the Iron Curtain had fallen by then. In Prague, they met Vaclav Havel, the president of the new Republic, and Shirley Temple Black, the US ambassador at the time. At the embassy one evening, they discussed literature over Pilseners, and Havel played his guitar for the guests. Dave's recollection of that visit is one of the most wonderful stories I've ever heard. Near the end of his enlistment, Dave met and married a smart and lovely Czech woman and they moved to Prague. The last I saw them, they were seated together at a small table in a Nürnberg café, and they waved me over and we drank beers and chatted. They were very happy together. I hope they are still happy.

When the transport ship carrying our vehicles arrived at Dammam, Dave and I stood at the wharf and looked out at the water. The sea blazed with sunlight; tankers dozed at the horizon. Dave said, affably disconcerted, "That's the Persian Gulf," and I laughed so hard I couldn't stand straight. The whole thing was hysterical. The ship came in and the vehicles rolled off. We painted them cat-shit yellow and drove them out of Dammam and into the desert.

Big Bend

In the shade of a stand of cottonwoods I found, as I'd hoped, a stream issuing from a spring. I washed in a foot of quick water and sat drying in the sun, long enough for the snipes to return to stalk the stream's edge and probe the wet sand with their beaks.

Late in the afternoon, I set up the tent and read a *Gedeones* Bible with interfacing Spanish and English text, a book I'd taken from a hotel room in Del Rio. This book is useful in my attempt to learn Spanish because I know the story, and I can follow the bread crumbs of a few known words.

La lámpara del cuerpo es el ojo; así que, si tu ojo es bueno, todo tu cuerpo estará lleno de luz.

As I read, I felt a dim thump in the base of my spine. Across the stream, five mule deer—four does and a buck—traversed the rocky face of the hillside. The does browsed, but the male faced me full on. He stamped his hoof and snorted for several minutes and did not move off, even after the females had departed. The hard ground conducted the hoof-stamps to me, a plain warning with which I'd have gladly complied were I not so tired.

The light of the body is the eye: if therefore thine eye be single, thy whole body shall be full of light.

The sun set and the world contracted to a patch of rocky ground hedged by black hills. I sat on a stone with a star chart and a flashlight wrapped in a sock to cut down the glare. It's been said that a thing, once named, loses potency. That's wrongheaded. There's Gemini. There's Sirius. Big Bear and Little Bear forever parted by the dragon. The Pleiades: the Seven Sisters riding the Bull's back, or, in a different story, the seven doves that nest on open ground, eternally untroubled by dangers. To the east stands Orion, who pursued them to this place. His arrow is pointed at them still.

Very late, several animals rushed past the tent, loosing strange cries. Javalinas, maybe. The Mexican gray wolf has vanished from this side of the Rio Grande, and coyotes keep their distance. Snakes and scorpions are here, but they're not very ambitious during the long winter nights. The fresh cold is conducive to sleep, and the sun will rise soon enough.

On the fourth day, I passed the miners' huts near the abandoned Mariscal Mine and camped at Elephant Tusk. Before dawn, I woke freezing and crawled out and kindled a small fire, boiled water for a coffee, rolled a cigarette, listened to the owl call from its roost on Talley Mountain. The moon set below the skyline. All that morning I hiked up into the Chisos, and I rested in the shade of junipers at noon.

After six days, I hiked down the Blue Creek Canyon, back to the highway. I was at the gas station, sitting on a curb eating a burrito, when James and Beth pulled up. They were on time, six days to the hour, just like they said they would be.

James grinned at me from behind the wheel. "He looks like he wants a beer." Beth had an open pounder of Budweiser in hand already. I tried to speak but my unused voice cracked, and they laughed at me. "Get in."

James and Beth were nurses. I'd met them some weeks earlier at Seminole Canyon State Park in Texas's Pecos River valley. They had taken a walk through the campground after sundown and had seen my tent, and my bike chained to a bush. At the time, I was intent on cycling from Austin to California, but the trip had been plagued with sleet and snow, and when they found me at Seminole Park, I was nearly finished. They asked if I wanted something to eat, and I declined; a few hours later, when the temperature dropped into the twenties, I reconsidered.

The scholar Hugh Kenner noted that "one has only to refuse a casual opportunity, and the curve of one's life commences a long slow bending away from what it would have been," and I've often refused such opportunities, out of misbegotten and outsize feelings of pride, fear of judgment, fear of disclosure or discovery, or plain self-consciousness. But that night in the Pecos valley, I made the fortunate choice to accept the kindness of strangers, and they welcomed me and fed me, filled my tin cup with good cheap wine, spread blankets on the bunk. In the morning they made breakfast and I loaded my bike on the RV's bike rack and drove with them to the Big Bend.

So I was not surprised, when I hiked out of the Chisos that day, to find them waiting at the appointed time and place. That night we sat on lawn chairs and drank beer, and I buried my feet in the sand to cool the blisters. We looked at the stars, talked about the places on earth we'd like to visit. They had recently given up their hospital jobs, sold their house, and auctioned their furniture with the intention of starting a market garden outside Kansas City. They'd already made an offer on five acres, they told me. It was a risky venture, an idea they had tended for a long time. They were happy.

A week after the hike at Big Bend, having imposed on their generosity for far too long, I said goodbye to them and pedaled north along US 90, which was reduced to one lane due to construction. When the road workers waved me through, a Texas Department of Transportation truck pulled out and paced me. When I slowed on inclines, the truck slowed; when I sped downhill, it accelerated. For fifteen miles, to the end of the construction zone, the truck kept a uniform lead. I cruised its wake at twenty miles per hour, just behind the orange tank that was mounted on the bed—a tar tank with black streaks feathering down from the spigot. Where the orange traffic cones ended, the driver turned off the road. He did not return my wave.

The highway split a level valley between the Sierra Blanca and the Sangre de Dios, mountains buried to the waist in their own talus. There was little traffic, no birds, only settled stillness. I felt conspicuous as the only body in motion for miles, like one traveling a condemned road. When the rear tire went flat, I poured water into the tin pan and fed the tube through, watching for bubbles.

I could not locate the puncture. The rock summits, varnished to coppers and cedars, hovered in the middle air, in the blue silence, and nothing moved in the creosote. Coyotes set up a cry that seemed both far and near, in the way sound travels over open water. I grew frustrated.

Fear, too, is a loss of compression. My lungs constricted as I knelt in the sand, there between the mountains, and the whole structure of the day began to slip. I found the puncture and patched the tube as the coyotes moved, both near and out of sight, orbiting like a planet.

I strapped the bags to the racks and pedaled hard, irritated by my lack of composure. Forty miles down the road I leaned the bike against a speed-limit sign and lay down in the littered grass beside the highway and slept.

I woke up thirsty and cold and stuck out a thumb. In the next town I would find some hot food, splash my face. A handful of raisins had no taste because I'd passed the stage of hunger into mere exhaustion. A truck hauling a horse trailer pulled onto the shoulder, and the woman stepped around the vehicle to meet me.

"Look, I don't normally do this," she said. "You look all right but I just gotta see some ID." I showed her my license, and we put the bike into the trailer, which had been fitted with a small table and a narrow bunk, the latter piled with black trash bags stuffed with clothing.

The sky had grown overcast while I was sleeping, the mountains had disappeared, and the featureless scrub ended vaguely in rain. As we set off, I asked her where she was from. "North Florida. My partner's a control freak. That's why I'm moving. He thinks everything's just gonna keep on going where it's going, and it ain't. I can't be around people telling me where not to go and what not to do. You know what I mean?"

When she dropped me off at the shop, she asked me if I needed any money. I pedaled on a few more days, but I'd lost heart in the ride. I didn't make it to California, not for several years.

The shooting war in the Persian Gulf in 1991 was over quickly, and the more I try to retain and recall events, the more unreliable the memories become. But I remember driving through the desert at night.

We drove without headlights, practicing what the US Army called "light discipline." Sergeant Haviland held a compass and a map in his lap, and I wore a pair of night-vision goggles, which revealed a moss-green world. In the months preceding hostilities, during the buildup of coalition forces in Saudi Arabia, we took long drives into the desert along the Saudi-Iraqi border, orienting ourselves and testing equipment.

One night, a glow in the sky burned up my night vision, and we arrived at a refinery complex the size of four city blocks. I took off the goggles and drove in. A many-tiered canopy of pipes, knotted with tanks and valves, rose around us; soaring metal stacks blazed like monstrous birthday candles; powerlines laced overhead, festooned with lights like strings of incandescent popcorn. A sinister desertion pervaded the place, as though it had been meticulously abandoned.

We passed through and entered the desert again, driving slowly as our vision readjusted to darkness. The place spooked me, and still does, like a vision of an untenanted future that somehow functions without us. The memory persists like a scrap of secret video, lacking audio, replaying to no purpose: a moving picture of waste fires whipping like outlandish flags, and gigantic undulant shadows.

The night-vision goggles were primitive things in 1991. They weighed two or three pounds, perched on the bridge of the nose, and gave me a murderous headache. One night, practicing light discipline, I stopped the vehicle and told Haviland that I wasn't wearing the damn things anymore. The only light in the vehicle was the green eye of the compass he held in his lap. Haviland lit on the idea of navigating by the stars. We worked out a system. He took a compass reading; I drove into the darkness. After a few minutes, I stopped, he took another reading, and I drove on. In this manner he guided me by slight degrees, compensating for error as we proceeded. *Little left*, he'd say. *Little right*.

The stars, and the dim green compass dial in Haviland's lap, were the only sources of light. I kept my foot on the gas, and we knew we were moving because the vehicle juddered violently. But the stars in the windshield remained fixed. That sensation of moving and not moving is a thing I can readily recall; it is one of my clearest memories of the Arabian Desert. I leaned into the wheel and fixed a star to a crack in the windshield glass and steered into it, peering skyward. The crack served as a sort of Jacob's staff, and I navigated truly by it, and it seemed I was performing an act of sorcery, like piloting a ship through Greenland fog.

Of course, the desert is not flat. There are clumps of bush and dry rainwash gullies called wadis, some of which are a few inches deep and some of which are deep and wide as riverbeds. We drove blind at twenty-five, thirty miles an hour, juddering in our seats until I was beaten careless, but I kept myself trained on the staff and the star. Haviland cupped the compass in his lap. Mike sat quietly in the back, listening, as we all were, to the rumble of the tires, waiting for the rumble to cease, which would signify that we had driven off a cliff.

Nikos Kazantzakis, referring to the Israelites, wrote that a people forged in a desert are indestructible. That's not always true. Consider the Sumerians, who invented the wheel and developed their own writing. Hammurabi's laws were written for them. They built pyramids called ziggurats, ceremonial monuments that have survived millennia. At the top of these ziggurats they sacrificed humans and animals. They were a powerful people. But the Sumerians are all gone, as are the Babylonians and the Assyrians and the Hittites.

After the ground war ended, we bivouacked for several weeks outside Nasiriyah, awaiting orders. No one knew where we were going next, and the endless speculation grew tiresome as the soldiers sat in the shade of the vehicles, dozing or playing cards.

I received a package from home one day with some books and a pair of running shoes, and I took off. After fifteen minutes of running, I stopped to check my bearings. Far behind, the company was a little jumble of trucks and antennae, a weird oasis swallowed in the enormity of the desert. After another fifteen minutes of running, I lost sight of them altogether, and I stopped. Suddenly the skyline presented a wholly unfamiliar aspect, and I heard nothing but my own breathing. I raced back after my own footprints, now blurred and seeming to lead in many directions, until I saw the vehicles again. I cursed my lack of nerve.

Over the next days I ran, each time a little farther, each time feeling a little more lost—but a bit less rattled, too—until the platoon sergeant put a stop to it. There were mines and unpoliced ordnance out there, he told me. People were still getting their feet blown off.

One evening while we were in that place, a dust storm appeared on the horizon, a great copper-colored wall of sand rolling like a leveler, bound directly for us. The soldiers in the company were from North Carolina, Illinois, Oakland, the Gulf coast, all of us ignorant of such phenomena, and we stood in the open to watch the storm's approach. Some retrieved point-and-click cameras from their packs and snapped pictures. It was surprising how quickly a thing that size closed the distance. Then I was on my hands and knees, cut off at a stroke, deafened and crawling toward the nearest tent, which materialized a foot from my face. I climbed in and found two others crouching there. The poles bent and the walls pressed in on us, but the stakes held. When the wind subsided, we emerged into the scoured light and saw that the storm, like a bandit colossus, had made off with some tents.

The regimental chaplain appeared one day, while we were killing time in that place, and asked if anyone wanted to learn something. We boarded trucks and rode to the ruins of Ur, the reputed birthplace of Abraham, the site of a ziggurat and the ruins of an ancient city. The chaplain, versed in history, led us through the excavated town whose narrow lanes were lined with brick. Shards of pottery littered the place. One shard sits illicitly on my bookshelf.

The chaplain showed us a dry well lined with tile, and bones embedded in the walls of domiciles, where the family dead were interred. We climbed to the top of the ziggurat, to the place of sacrifice. The horizon was equidistant at every compass point from the place where we stood. Dusty winds blurred the skyline. But for a few green streaks of irrigation canals, it is a dry and desiccated land. Here, finally, was the center of the desert, the last thing the victim would see. In this world, anyway.

When we climbed down again, I saw that someone had scratched a message with a sharp stone at the base of the ziggurat: KEVIN WAS HERE. Not me. A different Kevin.

The Cloud of Unknowing

I

On a deserted stretch of road, the taxi driver stopped the vehicle and gestured vaguely toward the empty horizon. "There," he said.

"Where?"

"There." Now I saw, or thought I saw, some irregularity in the distance, about a mile away: the reflection of standing water, or the attenuated shadow of a dip in the ground. After I paid the man, he sped off in a funnel of dust, and I began to walk.

No one standing a half-mile away would suspect the existence of this place, which was not so much a valley as a fissure in the earth, a mile long and a quarter-mile wide at the middle, tapering to a point at either end. Stone steps led down to a meadow rife with wildflowers, where a boy lounged in the grass and kept watch over a few sheep. A path led beside a tree-lined stream, beneath cliffs brimming with blue sky.

High on the cliff wall was the hermits' cave, abandoned a thousand years ago by Christian monks from Georgia, known then as Scythia. The interior of the cave was rounded and smooth, chiseled from soft stone. I found graffiti in Turkish, ashes and blackened stones from recent fires, some scattered trash. Also, frescoes of religious figures on the walls. The rich garments and outlandish eyes had faded into the rock with the passage of four thousand seasons.

I don't know why the monks created these images. Perhaps they are depictions of holy men, exemplars of fortitude and self-denial from the age of the Desert Fathers and Desert Mothers, ascetics whose names were legendary to the Georgian monks, but now wholly forgotten. Perhaps the images lent solace to the inmates during their interminable fasts and prayers.

Why did the monks come to this place? And was their little community sanctioned by the bishop at Ephesus? Perhaps they were a millennial sect awaiting the Messiah's return, or a zealous band inspired by the austerities of the Baptist whose voice, crying in the wilderness, led so many thousands into desert caves in those years. Perhaps they were dissidents, disgusted at the growing spiritual complacency of the Roman church, or fugitives from a decadent Byzantium whose days were numbered by a burgeoning Islam. Maybe they were women. Certainly, they did not want to be found. At least, not by people.

It seems such a sorrowful thing, to give up family, children, social regard, all that is valued by human beings. What did they accomplish? If the words of Jesus and Isaiah exhort believers to alleviate suffering, to serve the poor, to defend the widow and the orphan, then these monks forfeited their duties. Theirs was a pitiless courage, which identified self-denial with salvation.

They would have spent their days in prayer, begging mercy for themselves and for all people. They would have prayed for the fortitude to overmaster pride, knowing that all the ugliness in the world was rooted there. I've forgotten the name of that valley, somewhere in central or eastern Turkey, where I found the hermits' cave. I've looked through my notes and through travel guides in book shops, but I cannot find it.

II

I was pulled over on a highway in Missouri, just west of St. Louis, and arrested for possession of two pounds of marijuana. At the station, I was placed in a cell with a man who was wired on methamphetamine. He stalked back and forth, in an agony of withdrawal, as though he were trying to claw out of his own body. Shirtless, hyperventilating, he pumped his fists and sputtered like a man drowning.

Now and then, he recalled my presence in the corner of the cell, and I began to feel like an ugly and persistent reminder of something he wanted to forget, or something he wanted to break. At these times, I talked to him, as calmly as I could, about the uselessness of hurting me. I told him I was not his enemy, but he would not be placated, and I don't know if he understood a thing I said.

Over the next two hours, I found myself giving a reasoned argument for my own continued existence, which is a damned harrowing thing to have to do. I don't recall the premises on which I based my appeals. Probably, they were not very compelling in themselves.

Later, when I came to reflect on how unprepared I had been to justify myself, my case remained unpersuasive, even when I could assemble my argument at leisure. I came to think of those hours trapped with that tweeker as a live audition for that final interview, when we are haled before the throne to render an account of our days.

Two plainclothes officers led me to a small windowless room with a bare light strung from the ceiling and informed me that they knew all about me. At the time of my arrest, they told me, I was shadowing a large shipment of narcotics hidden in a white panel truck. If that truck happened to be pulled over, it was my job to turn off at the next exit, circle back, and run over the patrolman, thereby enabling the truck to get away. The story was so elaborate and absurd, I had to reassure myself it wasn't true. Several times I asked them to confirm the accusation that I had entered the state intending to kill police officers, and they answered *yes*. My denial only conferred legitimacy on the claim.

Over the following days, I was repeatedly brought from the cell to the room, where the same questions were put to me, though cleverly reformulated to catch me in a lie. Unless I supplied the names of those in the panel truck, the officers said, I faced up to fifteen years in prison for interstate trafficking. But I stuck to my story, which had the twin virtues of being easily recalled and almost true. I never had the smarts or the nerve to be a criminal or a dealer, but sometimes being honest is worse than useless. Of course, for most people in the world, that doesn't warrant mentioning.

A county parole officer named Mike came to visit. He asked me about my military service, which had shown up in the records, and he told me he had served in the army, too, and had also deployed to the Persian Gulf in 1990, though he never left the base in Kuwait. I thought I'd found a friend to whom I could appeal on the basis of shared service. I wrote a letter asking for his help, reminding him I was a first-time offender, a veteran. But he never responded, and I felt the shame and bitterness of having tried to parlay my military experience into some sort of leniency. No one, in fact, owed me anything for those years in the army, and I'd been a fool to expect otherwise. All I managed to do was cheapen one of the few things in life I can call my own.

Meanwhile, the intimidation game, grown tedious to everyone involved, came to an end. I pled guilty to Possession with Intent to Distribute—the only choice left to me after a series of bad decisions—and was sentenced to five years' probation and twenty-five days in jail. That's not a long time, just long enough to become acquainted with the eeriness of being shut up in a cage within a cage, where the incandescent light stains the skin and makes everybody appear ill. The pointless, unrecorded little cruelties—from guards and prisoners—that punctuate the hours, and the memory of a man dressed in a sleeveless orange jumpsuit, the payphone's receiver pressed to his ear, his head resting against the yellow cinder block, pleading for one last chance.

I've learned to be grateful for that little stint. I value it far above every other experience. It changed my mind about everyone and everything.

Because I had no connections to Missouri, my probation was transferred to Ohio, where I moved into an efficiency, worked part-time, got a library card, and stopped talking.

I daydreamed of absconding. In preparation, I checked out Spanish grammars from the library and listened to radio novellas from Panama on a Russian-made shortwave radio I'd taken from a blasted Iraqi bunker.

But even the sight of a city police cruiser made me nauseous, and I never summoned the courage to get away. Instead, I bought a bird guide and wandered the city parks. I rode the bus downtown and picked through the stones beneath the interstate bridges, looking for fossils, answering some strange impulse to categorize and index things.

Days passed during which I didn't exchange a word with anyone, except for the routine courtesies at checkout. I observed places and people more narrowly, and I felt a growing awareness of the despondency that pervaded the city. How a woman on the bus caught the eye of a child that was not her own, merely to convey a smile, and how the smile lingered over the oblivious child until the woman was visited by some hidden thought, and she looked away. How a young man leaned against the bus window, indifferent to what he saw outside, riveted on some inner pain, his face shadowed with an anguish that troubled me for days.

Everything struck me as flimsy, vandalized, and wicked. An effort had been made, it seemed, to cover up the true nature of things, but this deception only compounded the ugliness. People wore fixed expressions of fear, mistrust, despair. I hated all of it and wished for the whole thing to be razed to the ground. The city was rotten, society was rotten, and efforts to hide this fact were nothing but a malign pretense. I decided then to begin a program of study that would lead me to the source of this deceit. There must be, I thought, a time and a place when things began to go terribly wrong.

By proceeding methodically through the history of Western thought, through philosophy to theology, I would discover the roots of our spiritual fragmentation, the point at which truth had been fatally corrupted.

I began with the Greeks. I found quiet corners in the upper floors of the library and read the pre-Socratics. Democritus, who "would rather discover a single causal explanation than become king of the Persians." I recorded their strange admonitions in a notebook: "Wretches, keep your hands from beans!" and "Do not speak in the dark."

Moments of cheerful irreverence, too, I recorded. When asked why he had no children, Thales replied, "Because I love children."

Expressions of sorrow that seemed to have been spoken only yesterday. *I wept when I saw the undiscovered country.*

And the tender gravity in Alcmaeon's observation that "men die because they cannot attach the beginning to the end."

When I grew tired of reading, I wandered the stacks of periodicals, the reams of patiently compiled information in *Oil & Gas Journal* or *Minority Business Entrepreneur* or *US Catholic Historian*, shelves piled nearly to the ceiling, millions of hours of laborious notation and compilation, research, typewriting. I recall, in particular, paging through an issue of *Sky & Telescope*, from January 1985, and feeling nearly overcome by an immense futility. I read a few lines and put it back.

I was riding the bus one evening—uptown, downtown, crosstown, I forget—and thinking about the attributes of God, His self-sufficiency at violent odds with our insufficiency. This problem dogged me. How can perfection express love? And how can one love perfection? For the self-sufficient one, mercy and compassion are unnecessary. Human reason was calibrated to revere justice, not tyranny. Participation, not submission, was our proper mode. What more predictable and contemptible act can there be than to fall on your knees in the blinding light of the all-knowing and all-seeing, to kiss the hand of an indulgent master? No wonder the Israelites were so unfaithful.

"Where you going, sir?" the driver asked.

The bus idled at the curb, the seats were empty, it was dark outside. I'd missed my stop. I answered the face in the mirror above the windshield. "Is this the end of the road?"

"No, it's the end of the route," the driver said.

"I'm sorry."

"You sorry for what, child?"

There was a man. His name was Daniel. He wore a ring bearing a silver lion's head and he showed it to me: "Daniel from the lion's den," he said. He lived in the city park, and he panhandled along the streets of Corryville and Fairview Heights in Cincinnati. He wore a thick red beard and a wild tangle of red hair and in truth resembled a lion. Sometimes I bought him vodka or bought him a sandwich or gave him some money. At those times, he would weep into his hands and bless me and embrace me. He wore unwashed clothes, and the skin of his bare feet was split at heel and toe and covered with sores. His hands and face were filthy from rummaging in cans, living in the woods, sleeping in doorways. During the two years I knew Daniel, while I was killing time on probation, his mental and physical condition fluctuated day to day, but deteriorated over time.

He had difficult winters on the streets. I came across him once in the city park, deep in the gray woods, sitting on a disused bench, sobbing. When I sat beside him, he told me that some kids had destroyed his shelter and smashed his few belongings and burned them. It was cold. The police, he said, had knocked apart a rebuilt shelter. "My brother Jesus says I gotta forgive them seventy times seven times," he said. "And I done that. I asked my brother Jesus, 'Why do you let this happen? If you're with me, why do you let this happen to me?' But I forgave them. And still, there they are," he said, sweeping the bare trees with his finger. "Lurking. What am I gonna do, man? What am I gonna do?"

I went home and returned with a blanket and a coat, some pots and food, but he was gone. I left the things there and walked a long time.

Late winter, in February, when the sun might not shine in the Ohio Valley for weeks, I found him sitting in the gutter along a busy street. He was panhandling and I sat beside him and talked with him. A young man emerged from a deli and Daniel asked him for change. The man regarded the coins in his palm and tossed them, and Daniel spoke a blessing as he got to his hands and knees and picked pennies and nickels from the slush with swollen fingers.

In the spring, I began reading Frederick Copleston's *History of Philosophy* in nine volumes. I carried the books daily to the city park, where old men sat at intervals around the duck pond and kept a desultory watch on their slack fishing lines. In volume 2, part I, chapter 2, "The Patristic

Period," I read that "though man by nature has as his proper object of knowledge sensible things, these things are not fully real, they are mirage and illusion except as symbols or manifestations of immaterial reality, that reality towards which man is spiritually drawn."[1] The soul, therefore, "drawn by God, leaves its natural object of knowledge, without, however, being able to see the God to which it is drawn by love: it enters into the darkness, what the medieval treatise calls the Cloud of Unknowing." I read the passage twice, three times, went to the library, and found a worn copy of that medieval treatise, a 1961 Penguin edition translated from the Middle English by Clifton Wolters.

The Cloud of Unknowing was composed by an anonymous English priest in the fourteenth century. The style is earnest but unhurried, colored by moments of gentle emphasis. An earthy and optimistic tone, touched with irony, pervades the old scholar's encouragement of an eager but untested young man. A genial impatience with propriety combines with a kindly affection for youth to soften the gravity of the theme.

This work, the priest says, will be attended by loneliness and discouragement, but the novice is assured that, in times of despair, God in His mercy will descend "and take you up, and fondly dry your spiritual eyes—just as a father would act toward his child, who had been about to die in the jaws of a wild boar, or mad, devouring bears!"[2]

The book reveals no awareness of the wars and plagues that raged in those years, for these things, the author knew, would endure for as long as humanity endures. Didn't Jesus assure His disciples that there would be wars and rumors of wars? Even so. While the shadow of chaos looms over the horizon like an approaching weather front, the priest and the novice only concern themselves with the matter at hand, which is the question of how the young man might pass through the cloud of ignorance that separates him from God.

"In itself," the priest writes, "humility is nothing else than a true knowledge and awareness of oneself as one truly is. . . . Therefore strain every nerve in every possible way to know and experience yourself as you really are."[3] And when this is accomplished, a cloud of forgetting will gather between the world and the self that is consumed by sorrow, a desolation beloved by God.

> See to it that there is nothing at work in your mind but only God. Try to suppress all knowledge and feeling of anything less than God, and trample it down deep under the cloud of forgetting. You must understand that in this business you are to forget not only all other things than yourself . . . but to forget also yourself, even the things you have done for the sake of God.[4]

The kingdom, then, is the inheritance of those who disinherit themselves, as Francis did when he stripped in front of the mob at Assisi and handed over his costly garments. For the novice, this self-denial is compounded with the sorrow of departure, for in this new awareness of nothingness, he has severed himself from all he knows. Now, a deep forgetting has opened between himself and the world. From this point, despair is his sole companion, and he searches in vain for guidance and relief. He calls to God, but God is silent. This is what it means to be buried alive.

> This is that tyme of the whiche it is wretyn: Alle tyme that is goven to thee, it schal be askid of thee how thou haste dispendid it.[5]

Daniel began to run down during those days. I often found him unconscious, packed into a doorway of an abandoned storefront, a heap of damp clothes in bare feet. Then I would return to my apartment and think of the many times he had embraced me for some small kindness that cost me nothing. I thought, *I could invite this man home and feed him and give him a warm, dry place to sleep*. But always I fretted over what the neighbors might say, and what if the landlord found out? The law that governs such things, otherwise known as fear, overrode my conscience. So I never did.

The last time I saw him was a warm spring day. I was walking in the woods in the city park and found him seated on the ground, arranging french fries in a circle. He told me he was setting out the fries to entice his friends the squirrels to visit him. The branches were just then beginning to leaf. He arranged his fries, twelve of them, with trembling precision. "Twelve moons, twelve gods, twelve apostles . . ." He slumped forward and wept into his hands. "Oh god," he said. "How am I gonna feed my children like this?" I never saw Daniel again.

I found a poor and sick man. I left him in the cold and he disappeared and probably died, and a voice said to me, again and again, *I was a stranger and you took me in; I was naked and you clothed me*. I failed, and I was discouraged, because it is hard not to fail.

III

The novice does not speak directly in the pages of *The Cloud of Unknowing*, but his difficulties can at times be surmised. He must have protested the priest's enjoinder to stamp out "all remembrance of God's creation," for the priest repeatedly insists on looking for the truth that lies beyond language. Language is just so much signposting, the priest explains, devised to aid the traveler. It does not in itself reveal truth. That is the heart's business. As with any map, improper use will only complicate the journey.

> But what I will say is this: See that in no sense that you withdraw into yourself. And, briefly, I do not want you to be outside or above, behind or beside yourself either!
>
> "Well," you will say, "where am I to be? Nowhere, according to you!"
>
> And you will be quite right! "Nowhere" is where I want you! Why, when you are "nowhere" physically, you are "everywhere" spiritually.[6]

I read carefully but did not understand how the world might be benefited by a willing withdrawal from every living thing. It seemed cowardly, counterproductive.

The priest counsels inwardness and indifference to worldly values; thus disposed, we become most loving and generous toward—and most forgiving of—our fellow creatures. This turning inward, as I understand him, is really a turning outward.

> For the perfect contemplative holds no man as such in special

> regard, be he kinsman, stranger, friend, or foe. For all men alike are his brothers, and none strangers. He considers all men his friends, and none his foes. To such an extent that even those who hurt and injure him he reckons to be real and special friends, and he is moved to wish for them as much good as he would wish for his very dearest friend.[7]

But still I couldn't see how it was possible to live my life by these words. They remained perched on a high theoretical branch and would not come down. Godly sorrow and clouds of forgetting were abstractions that did not live to my mind as true ideas live. In order to fully realize these conceptions, a radical reimagining was necessary, but I was not able to achieve it.

> Moreover, the whole of mankind is wonderfully helped by what you are doing, in ways you do not understand.[8]

I returned the book to the library. Something did break through my dullness, though it wasn't what the priest intended. I came to suspect that the soul is an affliction, like homesickness, that a person is never fully at ease, not anywhere, for as long as they live. Maybe the soul could be defined, then, as the principle of disquiet, a fever as cureless as malaria.

"Alle men levyng in erthe ben wonderfuli holpen of this werk, thou wost not how."[9] After a few years, I checked out the book again, this time in the original English, and kept Wolters's translation at hand for reference.

I began to consider whether the ideas contained in the book were facets of a single, overriding sense of longing—longing for lost chances, or for love, or for some quiet space to breathe—which is the core condition of human life. And this longing takes the shape of an individual's response to another's suffering; or to the brief burst of color that catches the eye only as it fades; or to that unsought realization that intrudes on the workday, or late some evening, leaving me stranded inside myself. It is then that I recall my own voice arriving to my ears with a startling clarity—like sound that carries over water—with news about who I am.

A probation officer made unscheduled visits to my apartment. Officer Wick was a decent man doing a difficult job, and he showed me the kindness of treating me like a human being. With each visit, Officer Wick appeared more tired. The last time I saw him, I made a pot of coffee and we sat together at the table. He told me about the most recent case assigned to him, a fifteen-year-old who had murdered a man over money, a case that was much in the news at the time. The wreckage of the kid's life, and the collateral pain involved, grieved Officer Wick, and the sorrow was written on his face. He looked weary.

I told him that I was hoping to get away. He understood. "I got bigger things to worry about than you, no offense," he said, and he told me to stay out of trouble, to go do what I had to do. "Just don't let your name come across my desk." He thanked me for the coffee, we shook hands, and he left. And so my probation effectively, if not officially, came to an end.

IV

> Lat that thing do with thee and lede thee wherso it list. Lat it be the worcher, and thou bot the suffrer; do bot loke apon it, and lat it alone. Medel thee not therwith as thou woldest help it, for drede lest thou spille al.
>
> [Let that thing do with thee and lead thee whereso it list. Let it be the worker, and you but the sufferer: do but look upon it, and let it alone. Meddle thee not therewith as thou wouldest help it, for dread lest thou spill all.][10]

A year later, I pedaled north from the White Sands desert, through Albuquerque and the Jemez River valley, through rainy and snowy Colorado, and crossed into Utah. Coasting the long downhill toward Moab, I saw a sign for cheap lodging.

The hostel was situated behind the roadside warehouses in a mazy tract of cedar-shaded gravel lanes lined with small trailers that hadn't moved in years. The residents—underemployed rafting guides and transients and others on various forms of assistance—paid a small rent to the hostel owners. I settled for a dorm bed for ten dollars per night.

During the following days, I sat at the picnic table and read, or napped in the shade of an old tree. I didn't think to move on. Such a thought didn't seem to occur very often to anyone in that place. Few of the residents were bound to any schedule. Mornings, some went off to low-wage jobs in Moab, while others stayed behind to drink and smoke. It seemed to be a simple matter to wander into a place like this and never leave. You intend to stay a few days, and a few years later you're still there, drinking. I suppose there are worse decisions.

A woman ventured out of her trailer every day at noon. Gravely hungover, leaning on an aluminum walker, she made her way down the path between her place and the common kitchen. One morning, she paused to mash an anthill with the rubber tip of the walker's leg, cursing the victims' pertinacity in building their miserable town in her way. Her walker was festooned with colorful scarves and feathers, as well as stickers insulting to authority.

Her name was Beatrice Pendragon, and that was the name printed on her prescription bottles. One night in her trailer, we drank whiskey and smoked cigarettes. Clusters of pill bottles were arrayed on every level surface like so many loyal squads of mushrooms. She tried to pee into a plastic bottle but peed all over the carpet. She said she once dated Geezer Butler, bassist for Black Sabbath. She said she wanted to live, she said she wanted to die. I don't doubt but by now the issue has been resolved, one way or the other. I hope she has found some measure of peace.

For at the first tyme when thou dost it, thou fyndest bot a derknes,
and as it were a cloude of unknowyng, thou
wost never what, savyng that thou felist in thi wille
a nakid entent unto God.[11]

One night, a few residents sat drinking at the picnic table, talking about the Colorado River. I mentioned that I had never rafted white water before, let alone the Colorado. A man told me he might arrange something, but I didn't think much about it.

Late in the night, after most of the others had wandered off to their trailers and I was finishing my last beer, a young man stood up from the picnic table. He began to pace, and to talk. He had sat apart during the general conversation and had not spoken a word all evening. I'd met him here and there over the preceding week, but I had never seen him converse with anyone.

This, to the best of my recollection, is what he said.

A soul goes lost on the long journey to God. Having perceived, in the imagination of her heart, that the sensible world—the world we know by touch and sight—is not reality but a warped facsimile of reality, she disappears into intellectual darkness. In this suspended state of desolation she finds nothing to replace the old, false, comforting certainties. Now there is only nothing. She is trapped somewhere between the world, from which she is banished, and God, who remains hidden in darkness. This indeterminate middle ground that she is forced to wander is known by some as the dark night, and by others as despair. It is for her sake that Jesus called himself the man of sorrows, and sought other men and women of sorrows for his kingdom. Blessed are the poor in spirit, he told the crowd, for theirs is the kingdom of heaven, but few understood it then, and fewer understand it now . . .

I'd brought a paperback edition of *The Cloud of Unknowing* on the bike trip, Evelyn Underhill's translation this time. Perhaps this young man had seen it lying on the picnic table. I cannot otherwise account for the fact that he was speaking about John of the Cross, the soul's journey, and the people of sorrow. Maybe it was just a coincidence.

He paced back and forth as he talked, composing his words with his feet and hands.

During the night of despair, he continued, you must keep the divine vision always before you, in the eyes of the heart. Discipline and long-suffering patience are indispensable, because this night may last years. For many, the night never does end, and these poor souls will wander like Cain till the end of their days, trapped between heaven and earth, utterly alone.

When he finished speaking, he said good night and went to bed. An old man, the only other person besides myself who had remained listening, said to me, with mild astonishment, "That's the first time I seen that kid open his mouth."

In the morning, a truck pulled up, towing a raft on a trailer. Some of the residents had gotten hold of a boat and invited me to come along. "You said you wanted to do the white water, didn't you?" the woman said from the passenger seat of the idling truck. "You don't get to leave this place without rafting the river."

We rode the river, and as we bucked through a stretch of white water, I saw the guide like a fearless figurehead, one flip-flopped foot planted on the prow, a whiskey bottle and a paddle in either hand, shouting at the rainy clouds.

A few days later, I loaded up the bike and left Moab, crossed Glen Canyon, and pedaled the lonely road that winds through the juniper groves of Cedar Mesa in Utah until I arrived at the end of the world, which was not marked as such on my highway map.

At the southern edge of the mesa, the highway ends and the land drops a clean thousand feet, as though the earth has shifted by a single degree along its central plane, a catastrophic fraction out of true. The plain below rolled away to distant haze, studded with buttes and spires like a cosmic circuit board. The way down is a graded switchback called the Moki Dugway, a series of hairpin turns gouged from the cliff face. I paused for several minutes at the top, willing myself calm, hyperventilating and sweating as I looked down. My hands shook as I worried the cables and straps.

Then I rode my brakes down to the desert floor and passed Mexican Hat at a dead run. Singing out loud, I crossed the olive San Juan River that flowed quick and deep out of the mountains.

A few hours later, at a shoulderless stretch of state route, I thumbed a ride with a young Navajo couple. I sat in the truck bed with my back to the cab and a view of pavement unraveling in dust. The man wore a fedora with a turkey feather tucked at an angle in the band. The woman handed me a bottle of water and a piece of hard candy through the sliding rear window.

As we sped south toward Kayenta, my eyes watered in the windblown grit and straw. Someone changed the radio station, they laughed at a shared joke, and I'd have gladly ridden along to Tucson, or Oaxaca, or Uruguay if they were going that far.

Hell on Ducks

Wherever I turn my eyes I only see disaster and harshness.

—ERASMUS OF ROTTERDAM[I]

February

Pedaling into the wind was hateful. I cursed the wind, which was senseless. That only compounded my discouragement. On a state route in southeastern New Mexico, a constant headwind was attended by a steady drop in temperature. Late in the afternoon, I got off the bike and stuck out a thumb, hoping to catch a ride farther up the road where I might find some sheltering trees and wood for a fire. A sedan stopped but the driver had no room for the bike. He looked curiously at me when my voice cracked, gave me a bottle of water, and drove on.

As the sun set, I looked about for a place to pitch the tent. The crest of a nearby hill was crowned with a single wind turbine like a forgotten pinwheel, and the elemental hum of the blades filled the air. A pickup turned onto the shoulder.

"Had enough?" the driver asked. He helped me lift the bike into the truck bed, turned the heat up inside the cab, and handed me his business card: Triple AAA Used Cars. Truman Flowers, Proprietor. Anthony, TX.

He pulled off at the next exit to buy us a meal. "McDonald's okay with you?" he asked. "You don't look like you got a sweet tooth."

Truman Flowers was headed to Phoenix to check out some vehicles. Several times that evening, as we crossed the Chihuahuan Desert, he called his wife for a brief chat and concluded each call with a reassurance of love. Truman was seventy-six years old.

He talked about his son who was in and out of work, "hooked on junk" as Truman put it. He wasn't casting stones. "We all got our troubles," he said. "Hell, I drank for forty years. Being a man means knowing when to ask for help. It's a tough thing to learn and no one's gonna teach you how to do it. Believe me, I wasn't no good to nobody. Then I got me a woman. Don't be proud, I told him. My boy, I mean. You won't get far in this life being proud. Shit, that reminds me. I gotta call him up. Excuse me, young man."

Don't be proud. I'd heard it before.

When he wasn't in methadone clinics, Truman's son was roughnecking outside of Durango. He was in a bad state at present. Truman pleaded into the phone. "Look, son, you gotta get you a woman. I don't care if she's fat skinny ugly pretty. You need a woman. You ain't gonna do it alone. I know, I love you, too, boy. You know that, right?"

At one in the morning we stopped at a Motel 6 in Wilcox, Arizona. Truman wouldn't take any money for the room. He called his wife a final time and went to sleep.

"Look," he said at five the next morning. "I decided against Phoenix. I'm headed back to Texas. You gonna be okay?"

I was certain it wasn't the truth. He had taken me far enough toward California and didn't have the heart to tell me to get lost. I hadn't noticed my imposition and felt ashamed. I think he was worried that I had attached myself and might be difficult to shake. Riding in a heated cab was, after all, pretty nice.

Wilcox, Arizona, is part highway pit stop, part disused rail line depot. As I sat on a bench in the old part of town, clouds gathered on the horizon, the mountains dissolved in rain, and I made peace with a bone-deep disinclination to get back on my bike.

At the public library, I applied for a temporary card and looked at the job listings tacked to the bulletin board. There was an ad for a house painter. That'll do, I thought. Maybe I'll get a job and rent an efficiency behind Main Street. On Saturdays, I'll ride my bike out to the San Antonio Mountains—a woman told me there was a stream, high up in the mountains, that flowed through the cool pine woods. Few people ever visited the place, she said. On Sunday afternoons, I'll kill time at the bar beside the railroad tracks, watching football games while the last daylight filtered through the blinds. Maybe I'll meet a woman, like Truman had counseled. Maybe I could make some friends.

I spent the afternoon at the library, reading beside the window, and took the book back to the motel room in the evening. The next day I set a chair in the sun and read. The next day, too. I needed a break from cycling, is what I told myself. The Pakistani couple who ran the place charged only thirty dollars a night, but I was down to $150, and that was on my mind. I didn't worry too much about it, however, because spring had arrived in the desert.

At the laundromat I pulled a chair to the window. The old woman who dispensed detergent and coins came around the counter. "What book you got there, hon?"

It was a history of civilizations. The medieval scholar Ogyu Sorai, when asked what he did besides read books, answered that he liked to eat burned beans and criticize the great men of Japan. I told her that story and she laughed and said that the scholar must have been an old soul.

For three days I stayed at the motel reading the book, sitting in the sun, watching the mountains change color through the day.

I called James and Beth. They'd put a down payment on five acres, James told me over the phone, just like they said they would, and they could use some help on their farm. They could feed me, he said, but couldn't pay anything, so I boxed up the bike and bought a bus ticket with the last bit of money. They were waiting for me at the Kansas City Greyhound station.

The March weather was cold and sunny when we arrived at Tommy Thompson's farm, situated in rolling pasture and woodland sixty miles southeast of Kansas City. Tommy, a friend of theirs, had sold five acres to James and Beth, and they were now in the process of staking out the plots and making arrangements for spring planting. For the time being, while they finalized the purchase of a nearby farmhouse, the two of them slept in their RV in Tommy's driveway.

Beside Tommy's house was a stout red barn, and the three of them showed me to the loft where I would stay. Walls and floor of smooth planking, a bed covered in thick blankets, a mirror and a nightstand. A desk by the window overlooked a pasture where cows browsed. They left me there to stow my gear and I sat down at the desk that looked over the hills and the bare trees, and I was filled with gratitude, and regret, for a kindness that I could not repay.

I sent to my sister for books. Living at the farm, I thought, would afford me the time to pursue the ideas that had been dogging me.

One day, some guy who is neither old nor young, possessed of just enough reading to make him disagreeable, opens a book of Heraclitus's thought (or Nietzsche's or Thoreau's) and from that book he derives insights, the import of which, he thinks, have never occurred to anyone else in the world, and so presently he finds himself knocked up on philosophy. It's a common sort of trouble.

At the Farm, Warrensburg, Missouri

A neighbor arrived on a tractor and tilled the field, but the temperature remained too low to plant. In the meantime, we ran fencing: electric to keep out deer and cows, and mesh against rabbits. At night we gathered at Mary and Tommy's house to eat dinner at the big oak table. The five of us, and often a neighbor, ate and talked over mugs of beer. Tommy was a retired high school arts teacher. His wife administered hospice care to the dying. She herself had cancer and underwent treatments that robbed her of energy. But the talk was all about the future. Those evenings, when it was dark by six, there was a feeling that good things were afoot. My new friends included me in their plans, a rare joy in the average life, and one that must rank with food and shelter among basic human needs.

Because Beth had chronic back pain, James could use my help for the foreseeable future. Not that she wasn't tough. She left an abusive father at fifteen to marry an abusive man, and then found refuge, such as it was, in the marine corps. She made her own road. Once, when we were digging postholes along the road bank, James unearthed a five-foot King snake that had been sleeping away the winter. The thing writhed on the gravel road, cruelly roused from its slumbers. James called to his wife. She wrapped the snake gently around her waist beneath her coat, against her bare skin to warm it, and brought it inside. She kept it in their bathroom for a time and later, one sunny day, set it free beneath the house.

During meals, James and Tommy talked tractors, and Mary and Beth talked fruit trees, and I talked about the books I was reading. They laughed at the things I said, but kindly. After all, to mock philosophy, as Pascal wrote, is to philosophize truly. Their generous tolerance was my tuition, though I was often too selfish to esteem it.

As the days warmed, we planted potatoes and tomatoes. Onions: red, green, and white. Broccoli and spinach, cauliflower, carrots, and corn. After that, asparagus and strawberries and peach trees. At night, James and Beth read books and learned how certain flowers act as natural repellents to certain insects, so we planted rows of these flowers between the vegetables. They bought a dozen weed-eating geese called weeder geese that dutifully answered their eponymous callings. James planned to fertilize the rows with manure from the adjacent cow pasture.

When we heard birds, the work ceased. James pointed out a flycatcher with a seven-inch black-and-white tail perched on the wire. Indigo buntings arrived late that spring. Hawks in abundance: Cooper's, red-tail, rough-legged. The resident cuckoos, called rain crows in that part of Missouri, are the same that sing of the "visionary hours" in Wordsworth's poem.

Once, James called me over to see a small flock of cedar waxwings, all facing the wind, perched like Christmas ornaments in a young pine. They were the most beautiful birds I had ever seen, and I have never seen one since.

On the farm, I tried to develop an awareness for the bird life, but my ears and eyes were poorly tuned. The others, however, possessed a sixth sense for the sky.

This is Barry Lopez in *Crossing Open Ground.*

> It is the birds' independence from predictable patterns of human design that draws us to them. In the birds' separate but related universe we are able to sense hope for ourselves. Against a background of the familiar, we recognize with astonishment a new pattern.

I don't know what my friends thought of Lopez's observation. Perhaps they saw nothing unfamiliar, astonishing, or new in the patterns of bird life. Perhaps they would find in Sir Thomas Browne a more cheerful birder, who four hundred years ago noted that "the civilitie of these little Citizens more neatly sets forth the wisdom of their Maker."[2]

Phoebes nested above the door of Tommy's house. Baltimore orioles arrived, too. On one of Raleigh's (or maybe Dampier's) voyages to the New World, he recorded a description of a bird of great beauty, a scarlet bird with black wings. His men caught one and carried it back and presented it to the queen. And when I saw such a bird on the farm in Missouri, I realized that the sailors' gift was most likely a scarlet tanager.

Robins. Jays and chickadees. Several species of woodpecker—downy, hairy, red-headed, ladder-backed—lived around the farm, and on two occasions I saw the crow-sized pileated, a rare and shy bird. A series of descending *cuk*s announced his presence, then the low undulating flight across the cornfield. Big as a raven he was, black and white with a red cockade, like a guidon in the Kaiser's cavalry.

Wild turkeys entered their breeding season and paraded in a far-off meadow. At a mile's distance, the bronze iridescence of their tail fans was plainly visible.

Titmice and nuthatches, bluebirds. Thrashers and mockers. Barn swallows rifled in and out of the barn door.

These farmers kept bird guides and binoculars in the cabs of their trucks. The appearance of a hawk or a lark was a good excuse to pull over, or set aside a shovel. On the morning of the Audubon spring bird count, we woke at four in the morning and hiked the swamps and forests until evening. Tommy recorded his tally in a tape recorder and counted over one hundred species. Snowy egrets, great blue herons, a dozen kinds of duck. "If I see another dickcissel," I told them toward the end of that day, "I'll shoot myself." Tommy was dissatisfied with his duck-spotting skills. He compared himself unfavorably with a neighbor. "That guy," he said, "is hell on ducks."

An air force base is situated sixty miles from the farm, home to a different sort of bird, one that better resembled the mechanical birds in the mechanical tree at the Byzantine emperor's court. A person in the wrong place at the wrong time would have to be utterly dispirited to see an F-16 coming. As they pass, the jets emit a steel screech buried in a sonic roar, like a diamond hidden in a conch shell, and when they buzzed the place at three hundred feet, I thought the trees around me might drop to their knees. I recalled an overcast day in the Arabian Desert in 1991 when we knelt in the sand and watched a pair of A-10s dive on Iraqi armored vehicles, and how those aircraft seemed to shudder as the guns opened up, which was just a trick of the eye, I guess. The sound of a fighter-bomber on its approach is an outsize sound you feel in your gut, like standing beside a strong person snapping a carpet.

One day, when I was out by myself weeding potatoes, I sensed a change in the air. The B-2 Bomber was a three-acre-wide, tar paper–black wedge slipping noiselessly across the sky. The plane was overhead before the sound followed, but it did not appear to be going very fast at all, maintaining just enough thrust to keep from plummeting.

Our technology has the power to afflict like a dream—a dream that lingers too long and leaves the dreamer stranded in a haze of anxiety and ozone.

These days, despair looms over the horizon like the acoustic shadow of battle, but philosophy, I believe, is a bulwark, a shield, and a refuge at those times when it seems that even the simplest graces—forbearance, humility, decency, deference—have vanished from the earth. These are fragile things, after all, even in the best of times, perennially at a premium.

There's a story about the last days of the Academy in Athens during the sixth century of the common era. Plotinus and Proclus, who had sought to demonstrate how the individual soul was bound to the Divine Mind, were dead. Their followers preserved a tenuous existence amid a vigorous new religion that was consolidating its authority and growing increasingly intolerant of rivals. Within the walls of their beleaguered school, the philosophers nurtured their unitive vision in which the soul—after a long sojourn on earth, trapped in its carcass of clay—returns at last to its native ground. "For every one has all things in himself and sees all things in another," Plotinus had written in *The Enneads*, "so that all things are everywhere, and all is all, and each is all, the glory is infinite."[3] But the keepers of the new law subscribed to a radically certain faith; they had no taste for convoluted abstractions concocted by Greek mystics. In 529, the Christian emperor Justinian ordered the school closed. By then, as historian Rufus Jones writes, only seven scholars remained,

> and they took their beloved books and started out, from the famous seat of philosophy, to seek a quiet retreat in Persia—the wise men of the West going toward the East with no star for guide.[4]

While Tommy tinkered at his old tractors—vintage Alice Chalmers models that he restored and sold—he talked enginery, and sometimes he did me the kindness of asking me for a hand. One day, he set the tools aside and refilled his mug at the keg he kept in the barn. We sat on crates and watched the rain through the barn door.

He spoke of his first wife, who had died of cancer at a young age, and of her love of poetry. When the rain ended, we stood near the fence and he told me that, summer evenings, he and his wife came out here together, to the place we stood now, to watch the sun set and smoke a joint, a ritual they called the "children's hour." He missed her dearly and did not attempt to hide his grief.

Rain fell every day for some weeks, washing away a portion of the planting. I sat with a book at the window of the loft and looked out over the soaking fields and the solitary cows.

In 1486, the year Pico della Mirandola lamented that the study of philosophy had come "to despite and contumely,"[5] Erasmus of Rotterdam was twenty years old. He was soon to take vows as a canon of the Augustinian Order (to which his future nemesis Martin Luther also belonged), but Erasmus was a half-hearted monk at best, and he made a career of avoiding his post at the monastery at Steyn, choosing instead a wandering scholar's life and a reliably precarious living as tutor, editor, secretary, and author. His famous work, *The Praise of Folly*, earned him more suspicion than money. A settled situation was offered to him more than once during his life, but he had a constitutional aversion to commitments that might detract from his studies. "On no other account," he wrote, "do I congratulate myself more than on the fact that I have never attached myself to any party."[6]

He resented the necessity of earning his living, since it took him away from his studies, and he complained of poverty all his life. But time and again, when presented with lucrative positions in the church that promised to allay his financial worries, he declined and chose instead the irregular income brought by writing—supplemented by much judicious wheedling of wealthy admirers:

> . . . plead my shyness before my Lady in pleasant phrases, as if I had not been able to bring myself to reveal my poverty to her in person . . . unless indeed you are so superstitious that you scruple to employ a few harmless lies to help a friend.[7]

Fastidious, prone to illness and hypochondria, he detested noise and disorder, and though he hated contention, he could be indifferent to cruelty, as evidenced by his casual anti-Semitism. His lack of a fixed abode did not, however, seem to trouble him. A loyal correspondent, he had friends throughout Europe who largely tolerated his many importunities. Europe presented few linguistic or political boundaries to the educated Christian man, and he was restricted only by his personal antipathies for Dutch drinking habits and the excessive heat of German kitchens.

> We had supper in a small room like a sweating-chamber, more than sixty of us, I should say, an indiscriminate collection of rapscallions, and this went on till nearly ten o'clock; oh, the stench, and the noise, particularly after they had become intoxicated.[8]

Europe in the early years of the sixteenth century seemed to Erasmus to be witnessing the dawn of another Golden Age. Humanists like himself were promoting the ancient learning, reviving Greek letters, and restoring the early Latin Fathers to their original clarity. This dissemination of the "good learning," well underway in Italy, would put an end to discord and senseless scholastic disputation and would nourish universal reverence for the ancient virtues of tolerance and moderation (at least, so far as these ideals were then conceived).

In 1516, referring to the enlightened princes of England, France, and Germany, he wrote the following to Wolfgang Fabricius Capito:

> It is to these men's piety then that we owe it that all over the world, as if on a given signal, splendid talents are stirring and awakening and conspiring together to revive the best learning. For what else is this but a conspiracy, when all these great scholars from different lands share out the work among themselves and set about this noble task, not merely with enthusiasm but with a fair measure of success, so that we have an almost certain prospect of seeing all disciplines emerge once more into the light of day in a far purer and more genuine form?[9]

Even "the Scots, the Danes, and the Irish," he added, had embraced the good learning. In this atmosphere, the true Christian spirit of love and forbearance would thrive, and men and women of all nations would find refreshment and edification at the purified springs of knowledge.

A commonwealth of philosophers, poets—book lovers, all—existing in concord and mutual respect, knowing war no more. Erasmus himself would pave the way. A thorough emendation of the Greek New Testament would provide the foundation for an updated Latin version. Over the centuries, the Vulgate had grown turgid with bad Latin and the commentaries of wooden-headed monks. These errors were intolerable. There was no time to waste, much work to be done. Clarity was the watchword. Who would cavil at the necessity of restoring Saint Paul to his native eloquence?

A year after Erasmus had written so hopefully to Capito, Luther composed his Ninety-Five Theses, and the world came crashing in. Erasmus, deep in his studies, seems to have misunderstood the terms, and then underestimated the gravity of the conflict. He insisted that the controversy could be settled by a working knowledge of Greek and a dose of Christian charity. But the troubles concerned more than exegetical matters and the legitimacy of sacraments. Church revenues and national sovereignty—money and politics—came into play in ways that failed to register with the bookish Dutchman. His conciliating disposition made him supremely unfit for the new world, which belonged, and had probably always belonged, to brawlers like Luther.

"Wild beasts can be tamed by kindness," he wrote to the archreformer in May 1519. "More can be done by unassuming courteousness than by violence."[10] When the true shape of things finally became clear to him, the scholar again pleaded to Luther that "the essentials of our religion are peace and unanimity. . . . These can hardly exist unless we make definitions about as few points as possible and leave many questions to individual judgement."[11]

But it was too late for all that.

Erasmus, unable and unwilling to abide Luther's vulgarity or dim view of human destiny, refused to confront the issue on those terms. Trapped between the dogmatic Keepers of the Law in Rome, and the dour predestinarians in Switzerland and Germany, Erasmus chose a middle way. Then, as now, it was a lonely choice. And so the world "thunder[ed] past him," historian Johan Huizinga wrote, "disdaining his ideal of moderation and tolerance."[12]

He spent his last years in Basel and Freiburg, editing Chrysostom and Jerome, as hostilities spread. An image of Erasmus's final days comes from Beatus Rhenanus, who describes the old scholar seated at a desk, rereading friends' letters and repeating to himself, "This one, too, is dead."[13] The Pope tried to enlist him in the great struggle; Erasmus politely declined.

Christopher Eschenfelder was a customs official at Boppard in Germany, whom Erasmus had befriended on one of his travels.[14] Eschenfelder asked Erasmus to dedicate a commentary of one of the Psalms of David to him. Having forgotten whether Eschenfelder had specified a psalm, Erasmus chose the fourteenth, which begins with these words:

{To the chief Musician, A Psalm of David.}
The fool hath said in his heart, There is no God. They are corrupt, they have done abominable works, there is none that doeth good.
The Lord looked down from heaven upon the children of men, to see if there were any that did understand, and seek God.
They are all gone aside, they are all together become filthy: there is none that doeth good, no, not one.
Have all the workers of iniquity no knowledge? who eat up my people as they eat bread, and call not upon the Lord?[15]

It was his last composition.

I see him clearly, poring over his Greek manuscripts in a freezing room, a solitary man convinced that what the world needs more than anything right now is a new translation of Basilius's commentaries on Isaiah. That futility, that failure—even after five centuries—has the freshness of new-mown hay.

Cool and abundant sunshine attended the first day of the arts and crafts fair, a yearly event Tommy organized at the farm for the benefit of local artists. That morning I took a walk through the neighboring woods and fields. A breeze plaited the tall brown grass. The blue shadows of clouds darkened the pines' crowns passingly and grazed the muddy fields of hacked cornstalks.

A coyote, large as a police dog, flushed and fled in a mottled copper coat. I didn't know what the coyote was doing there, lying hidden in the grass. Maybe a coyote sometimes just wants to lie in the warm sun and be left alone.

I returned to the farm and found the place busy with cheerful preparations. Dozens of cars and trucks lined the lane. James and Beth set up a booth and gave away green onions—the first food we had harvested—and some literature concerning the planned co-op. Sculptors, painters, woodworkers, and potters arranged their wares on folding tables. Banjos played. A couple came down from Kansas City and set up a barbeque.

A woman named Teresa sold clay tablets the size of playing cards, each painted with an image of the Mexican Day of the Dead. I bought a glazed tablet bearing the image of a skull, *La Calavera* printed along the bottom.

Teresa was a flutist and a Spanish teacher in Kansas City. Her husband had recently died from a long and painful illness. She was left alone in a house she could not keep up with, so I agreed to borrow Tommy's pickup the next weekend and drive out to do some yard work.

In a tidy little study, her husband's books still lined the shelves, and she wondered what she would do with all his things. She gave me one of the books, Carl Becker's *The Heavenly City of the Eighteenth-Century Philosophers*. While Teresa was out running errands, I swept the sidewalks and pulled weeds, then sat in the study with the shades drawn and read about Madame Manon Roland, who kept a salon attended by the intellectual stars of the day.

Madame Roland felt stifled. She was steeped in the classics and Rousseau's philosophy, and she resented not having been born a Roman. The barbarities of the Revolution disgusted her. "Where could she converse with those who would understand her," Becker asks, "where do heroic deeds or make sacrifices that would not go unrewarded or unacclaimed? Not in the real world of Paris, but in the world of history, in the world of Plutarch and Jean Jacques, in the world of the imagination: there was a world in which others might see her as she saw herself."[16]

She wrote her memoir in prison. "O Liberty," she wrote, shortly before she was led to the guillotine. "What crimes are committed in thy name!" Soon after her execution, her husband Roland killed himself.

The temperature approached one hundred degrees outside, for it was July in western Missouri, but it was cool and dark in the house that day as I looked over her husband's poetry books. His tastes ran to the formal and he had the habit, as I do, of underscoring lines that spoke to him, or troubled him, and I paused at those words and phrases that had refused, for some reason, to be passed over.

This line of a poem was set off in penciled brackets: *Then what I am afraid of comes.*

But I cannot recall the name of the book or the author.

A Brief History of the Huron

It might seem that this persistence of the past could do no harm. What does it matter if all dead things still exist, so long as they remain safely enclosed, like a city under the sea? But this is not the case. The irremediable presence of the past darkens human life, and reaches out to determine it.

—J. HILLIS MILLER, *The Disappearance of God*

I

The neighborhood was under construction then. I scoured the half-built houses for refundable pop bottles and cans discarded by the roofers and framers. Sunday mornings, I filled a sack with empties, arranged the cans on the driveway at home, and stomped them one by one till my socks turned tacky with sour beer and cola. Each empty bottle brought me a dime closer to Francis Parkman's *History of France and England in North America*, the two-volume Library of America edition with Prussian blue, silk ribbons for page-keepers. The set cost forty dollars, or a couple thousand cans, or several hundred bottles. I grew anxious and mulled schemes to swindle the History Book Club, which would doubtless sell out of copies long before I could steal enough loose change to buy my own.

There were maps in those books, the catalog affirmed, reprints of the very maps that Parkman consulted during his research. Maps of the Ohio valley and the Pennsylvania frontier—elegant maps, spare and unadorned—depicting big rivers bristling with tributary streams that traced back into uncharted forests where the Oneida fished and hunted bear, where the Tuscarora burned their Huron captives, and where the Flemish Bastard and his renegades made their winter camps, there to drink and plot the next raid on the settlements.

I got the money together. On the day the books arrived, I bought a Hershey's chocolate bar at the convenience store, returned home dizzy and exultant, sat down at the kitchen table with a glass of milk, and opened volume I, *Pioneers of France in the New World*, chapter I, "Early Spanish Adventure, 1512—1561," which chronicled the expeditions of Narvaez, de Leon, and de Soto. I restrained myself from racing down the page. To read with patience and understanding was agonizing. "Nor is it surprising," Parkman wrote of the Spaniards,

> that amid such waking marvels the imagination should run wild in romantic dreams; that between the possible and the impossible the line of distinction should be but faintly drawn, and that men should be found ready to stake life and honor in pursuit of the most insane fantasies.

Hours passed. I looked up from the page to see my dad watching me from the doorway. "Everything all right?" he asked.

In the mid-1990s I worked as a plumber's apprentice in Cincinnati and attended plumber's school at night. The journeyman I worked with was a man named Derek. Broad-shouldered, mid-thirties, dark good looks inherited form his Italian immigrant mother, Derek was a kind man with a generous and disarming nature, and for this reason he was well liked by the office secretaries and by the other tradespeople. I'd never seen a father show such unabashed joy in his children, two girls. His wife was the only woman but one, he told me, that he'd ever slept with. A man generally wouldn't confess to such a thing if it weren't true. He was honest like that. Imposture simply didn't occur to him.

Here's an example. A friend of his was killed in a work accident. On the way to a job one morning, we stopped at a cemetery. For a few minutes, he stood in the rain beside the turned earth of the grave, and he remained quiet throughout the day. After work, back at the shop, he wanted to talk about the dead man, but when he brought up the fact of visiting the grave, the other workers ridiculed him, and a hurt look came over Derek's face, an angry hurt.

That kind of person.

I arrived at the shop one morning—normally a glum place at that hour—and found Derek happily recounting a story to two plumbers. He was not much of a reader, but someone had given him a book, and he'd been carried away by it. He was talking about the swamp-fighting in South Carolina during the American Revolution. I knew the story, and the book's title.

"Francis Marion, *Swamp Fox of the Revolution*," I said.

Derek was astonished, warily so, as though I'd read his mind. "How the hell did you know that?" I didn't tell him that it was the first book I'd ever read on my own, when I was a kid at Saint James Elementary. For me, it was a wonderful coincidence, but I didn't say so.

Derek embarked on a book jag. He read books about local history, about the Miami and the Shawnee, about the arrival of the French and English in the Ohio River valley. As we drove the unmarked van around the city from job to job—sweating water pipe, cutting away disused cast iron at a tear-out job, boiling lead in iron ladles in murky crawl spaces—we talked about the Jesuit Marquette's voyages; about gauntlets and ordeals; about the indefatigable LaSalle who paddled the lengths of the Mississippi and Ohio Rivers, both up- and downstream; about Little Turtle, brilliant strategist of the Miami, whose confederacy crushed St. Clair's army on the banks of the Wabash, inflicting the bloodiest defeat ever suffered by the American military at the hands of Native Americans. We talked about prisoner exchanges and broken treaties; captivity stories; the vanished buffalo of the "Cain-tuck" hunting grounds, the great herds that today survive only in a mural painted on the levee wall on the Newport, Kentucky shore. We talked about Blue Jacket, who, according to a suspect legend, was a white child adopted by the Shawnee. It was Blue Jacket's men who routed General Harmar's army from Ohio and Indiana. He was present, too, at Fallen Timbers in 1794, by which time the

Americans—with time, men, and money on their side—had learned the strategic value of burning the tribes' fields and towns.

We talked about trees.

Like the stage set to a gothic drama, in solemn attendance at every chapter of that history, were the enormous woods. We returned to those vanished forests gladly and often, if only in workday talk. The forest was a terror and a mystery for most Europeans who, unlike this continent's first peoples, possessed a constitutional aversion to wilderness. The complex canopy, hundreds of feet high, filtered the sunlight to variable shades of violet. Summers, the combatants and the wandering bands must have blinked like moon-people as they emerged from the gloom to rest beside some sunstruck river or lake. In winter, more natural light fell on the paths, but by then the ways were deep in snow, and travel was agonizing for those unused to snowshoes.

The forests of Ohio were axed and burned long ago, and the memories of nations have largely departed with the solitude of the great woods. By taking thought, I can imagine those trees, but to my mind they only ever appear dim and half-unreal, rooted in abstraction. What remains of the old-growth forest in Ohio would fit into an area the size of a county park.

History is not an American pastime. This is partly due, I think, to the fact that history has long been presented to schoolchildren as a thing from which they are meant to draw "lessons," as though history were a series of unfortunate incidents involving hot skillets and monkey cages, which, in some ways, I suppose it is. The past is something that maladjusted people "dwell on," after all. "The belief that history has a present use when properly read," wrote Jacques Barzun in *From Dawn to Decadence*, "is a mark of the modern temper; whole periods and peoples have done quite well without it," and that seems true enough.[1] Remembrance is morbid, unprofitable. It's impractical, impolite in certain company. And plainly, we survive whether we record our deeds and disasters for posterity, or we don't.

James Wright wrote a poem titled "In Response to a Rumor That the Oldest Whorehouse in Wheeling, West Virginia Has Been Condemned." A boy is hiding in the "hobo jungle weeds" along the Ohio River. There he is struck by a vision of women, purses swinging, walking without fear into the water like so many Ladies of the Lake. Emerging on the other side, "beyond death," the women will find, not the golden shore of promise, but Bridgeport, Ohio.

Someday, no doubt, I'll also step ashore at Bridgeport. I wonder if I'll meet the drowned prostitutes of Wheeling there, or Narvaez's soldiers, or the ghosts of Pottawatomie women wandering the banks, stranded beyond death. Perhaps I'll find the place deserted but for a stray playing card and a few blackened stones. I don't know. I've never been to Bridgeport, nor has anyone ever returned from there. But just in case, I should bring a small gift along. A goose feather, a holey stone, some flower whose name I'll certainly mispronounce.

It's easy to conceive of the dead as a forgiving crowd, but I'm not so certain. The German poet Heine wrote that God will forgive us, because that's His métier. But the dead labor under no such obligation.

Scattered up and down the Ohio, Scioto, and Miami River valleys, the sites of historical significance were long ago effaced by tractor and leveler. Here and there, a roadside marker bears the name of a trading post or a treaty site or a vanished Shawnee town. Beyond the sign may be an onion field or a deserted lot or a busy street corner, and the passerby who bothers to read the sign might try to reimagine the scene. It's difficult to do. Modern society has re-created the land in its image, and the land seems to have turned inward, like a prisoner who's been tormented and beaten but still refuses to talk.

Heraclitus made the curious observation that Nature loves to hide. History, too, loves to hide. The closer you look at the land, the more it conceals, and so the past becomes an unlikely, semi-mythical, inscrutable place. Only shadows and erasures and faint prints remain of the life that this land's first inhabitants knew.

When I was a kid, I was aware of the presence of ghosts. I had an inborn talent for paying attention, which compensated in a small way for my ignorance. Then, sorrow and love were indistinguishable, and together these constituted a kind of key to a passing knowledge. I mean to say that, innocent of judgment, I was permitted to listen, and to look. Things lay unconcealed to me then that are now hidden in plain view. I'm older now, lazy, judgmental; the key is lost.

When I was a kid, history books had this in common with the moon at two in the morning: both had a way of making me feel as though I were the only soul in the world who was watching.

II

From the early seventeenth century, the Huron had represented the Jesuits' best hope of establishing an empire in the wilderness. The Order had dedicated tremendous resources over many years to Christianizing the Huron, who were geographically most accessible and were deemed, due to their long familiarity with the French, most amenable to mystifying news of the creator's self-revelation. Once the Huron were converted, the Jesuits reasoned, the other tribes would see the good that came from renouncing war and pantheism; the nations would fall like dominoes before the cross, and the fleur-de-lis would wave in triumph over the primeval forest. Then the priests would turn their attention to those demons the Iroquois, and only then would the great battle—the Armageddon for the soul of the continent—commence. After half a century, however, of exertion and privation, the Jesuit investment had yielded only a few scattered camps of half-starved converts, and a growing honor roll of martyrs.

Among the Europeans who came to this hemisphere were figures whose imperial ambitions were celestially sanctioned. A breed of schizophrenics: murderers possessed of poetic eloquence; fanatics who gladly laid down their lives for strangers. This split-mindedness was a symptom of an age when the medieval and the modern were struggling for mastery—not only for western civilization, but also for individual souls. The mixture proved volatile, as the life of Luther proves, and could produce, if not monsters, then men with monstrous energies.

I was awed and appalled by the likes of them, as they were revealed in Parkman's books, for they seemed larger than life. I never crossed a bridge over the Miami or the Ohio Rivers in the family car without imagining Shawnee traders or toque-capped voyageurs or black-robed priests paddling canoes below, visions that vanished at the first glimpse of a limestone barge, or trash from old floods fixed like bunting in the trees.

At the watershed of the late medieval and the early modern periods, the Western mind was, for good or ill, more capable than now of accommodating mutually exclusive certainties.

The first four books of *France and England in North America* concern the settlement of New France. It is the story of Hurons and Iroquois; of Dutch rum and gun runners; of Spanish pillagers and French explorers and a multinational struggle for control of a devastating trade in beaver pelts fueled by a faraway craze for hats; of Scottish soldiers and English colonists eking out a precarious existence through miserable Pennsylvania winters, tilling the stony ground with their matchlocks on their shoulders, ever alert to raiding parties. And through this tale runs, like a strand of black thread, the story of the Jesuits.

> The Jesuit was, and is, everywhere,—in the school-room, in the library, in the cabinets of princes and ministers, in the huts of savages, in the tropics, in the frozen North, in India, in China, in Japan, in Africa, in America; now as a Christian priest, now as a soldier, a mathematician, an astrologer, a Brahmin, a mandarin, under countless disguises, by a thousand arts, luring, persuading, or compelling souls into the fold of Rome.[2]

Confronted with the possibilities of the New World, the English Protestants gradually exchanged their inherited hierarchies for a degree of self-determination. The Jesuits, in their scattered Canadian missions, suffered no such change of heart. Physical life was radically altered by the severe terms of survival, but the soul never quite cut free from French soil, or from Rome, or from the world to come. "Those who shaped the character," Parkman writes,

> and in great measure the destiny, of New France had always on their lips the nothingness and the vanity of life. For them, time was nothing but a preparation for eternity, and the highest virtue consisted in a renunciation of all the cares, toils, and interests of earth.[3]

When the friars disembarked at Montreal after the voyage from France, they carried with them precise instructions from their superiors in Paris concerning their comportment during the voyage up the Ottawa River to their duty posts. Parkman here translates and summarizes the "Instructions for the Fathers of our Company on the way to the Huron":

> You should love the Indians like brothers, with whom you are to spend the rest of your life.—Never make them wait for you in embarking.—Take a flint and steel to light their pipes and kindle their fire at night; for these little services win their hearts.—Try to eat their sagamite as they cook it, bad and dirty as it is.—Fasten up the skirts of your cassock, that you may not carry water or sand into the canoe.—Wear no shoes or stockings in the canoe; but you may put them on in crossing the portages.—Do not make yourself troublesome, even to a single Indian.—Do not ask them too many questions.—Bear their faults in silence, and appear always cheerful.[4]

After the journey up the Ottawa, the priests divulged to assembled villagers their visions of a Christian empire where French and Indian lived together in peace and prosperity. Official histories record the priests' astonishment at their hosts' prodigious memories as well as their selflessness. The Huron were much given to dancing and to practical jokes, and they dwelt with good humor and resilience within narrow margins of survival. Stinginess was the one unforgiveable sin.

> Among the Iroquois and Hurons . . . there were marked distinctions of noble and base, prosperous and poor; yet, while there was food in the village, the meanest and the poorest need not suffer want.[5]

To the Huron, the French were a mystifying species, "marvelous in knowledge, careless of life."[6] They could not fathom the good fathers' scorn for the passing joys of food, dance, and sex. The priests were welcomed in good times, tolerated in lean times. Their proven courage carried much currency among their hosts and spared the Frenchmen's necks when the Huron were tempted by hunger to rid themselves of unproductive dependents.

The Jesuits continually, and with limited success, implored the Huron not to burn or torture the prisoners who fell into their hands, but on one occasion these practices supplied the priests with a fitting illustration of the creed they expounded:

> "You do good to your friends," said [Father] Le Jeune to an Algonquin chief, "and you burn your enemies. God does the same."[7]

The Huron were, to the Jesuits' happy surprise, often amenable to visions of Paradise and the One True God, but the obscurer notions of redemption and perdition seldom withstood scrutiny.

The Huron were enjoined by custom to maintain a high tolerance for these uninvited fanatics. However, despite an honest desire to accommodate their guests, they could not wholly suppress their instinctive skepticism. At these moments, the Huron came to life on the page, for their humor was to me a familiar mix of mock obtuseness and downright irreverence, and in their words I heard the voices of my un-mystical neighbors, the German Catholics of Cincinnati's west side, with their inborn leeriness of other worlds. "With respect to the advantages of the French Paradise," Parkman wrote, the Huron "was slow of conviction."

> "I wish to go where my relations and ancestors have gone," was a common reply [to the Jesuits]. "Heaven is a good place for

> Frenchmen," said another; "but I wish to be among Indians, for the French will give me nothing to eat when I get there."
>
> "Which will you choose," demanded the priest of a dying woman, "Heaven or Hell?" "Hell, if my children are there, as you say," returned the mother.
>
> "Do they hunt in heaven, or make war, or go to feasts?" asked an anxious inquirer. "Oh, no!" replied the Father. "Then I will not go. It is not good to be lazy."[8]

The Jesuits prayed for patience for themselves, enlightenment for the heathens, and persevered. "Send me," wrote the priest Garnier in a letter to a correspondent in France,

> "a picture of Christ without the beard." Several Virgins are also requested, together with a variety of souls in perdition—*âmes damnées*—most of them to be mounted in a portable form . . . Of souls in bliss—*âmes bienheureuses*—he thinks that one will be enough . . . The colors should be bright; and there must be no flowers or animals, as these distract the attention of the Indians.[9]

The friars were occasionally killed or driven off. But slowly, imperceptibly, over the toilsome years, a community of converts began to grow. Their annals record every moment of visionary transport, every act of tender care for the aged, the infirm, and the dying prisoner. Word of an infant succumbing to plague would compel them in any season on long journeys with a vial of holy water and perhaps a few drops of chrism. They hoped to die alone in the forest, in the service of souls, drowned in a cataract, or cut down on a lonely path, for by such means lay the surest route to redemption, and privation and pain represented powerful sureties against their own miserable sins.

When the first Ursuline nuns disembarked at Montreal, at the end of a summer afternoon, the priests took pains to welcome them. "The sun sank behind the western forest," Parkman writes, "and twilight came on.

Fireflies were twinkling over the darkened meadow."[10] The priests caught the fireflies and tied them to sewing thread to festoon the branches and the altar withal.

There is an incident from this chronicle, which took place when the Huron faced extinction at the hands of their enemies, that has remained in my mind. It is an incident purely inconsequential of itself, and I'm not certain why Parkman chose to preserve it. It is the vision of Father Brébeuf.

> Once, when he was among the Neutral Nation, in the winter of 1640, he beheld the ominous apparition of a great cross slowly approaching from the quarter where lay the country of the Iroquois. He told the vision to his comrades. "What was it like? How large was it?" they eagerly demanded. "Large enough," replied the priest, "to crucify us all."[11]

Thirty years after I read of Brébeuf's vision, I encountered a similar story recorded in another book, Edmund Blunden's *Undertones of War*. In his account of his years in the trenches during the First World War, Blunden recalls a strange apparition. His "poor, dear platoon" were out stringing barbed wire when "a wisp of vapour was seen by my working party to glide over the whole sky from west to east, preserving all the time a strange luminous whiteness and an obvious shape, as some said, that of a cross, as others antipathetically held, of a sword, then there was a subdued conversation about it, which spread from man to man."[12]

The implications of some awful mystery, one that has its source deep in western memory, reveal themselves, at long intervals and in awful forms, to common souls in moments of uncommon distress. Death is cruciform, like the human body, like the tree of pain, and has appeared on at least two occasions: once, over three centuries ago, to a Jesuit priest in the Canadian woods, and again to a platoon of Royal Sussex riflemen in France in 1917.

Christianity is a religion of death and for centuries derived its authority from the power of death, and from the fear of death. But among Christians there has been a long turning away from these dark matters, a sea change coincident with Christianity's long decline. Brébeuf's talent for severer visions, a gift for perceiving specters, though common in his day, is rare in ours. The noise of the world has degraded that faculty. I suppose we should be grateful.

Banished from the Old World to the New by nationalism, by rising wealth and a burgeoning individualism, by Renaissance and Reformation, the medieval spirit endured for another century in the forest that stretched between the Illinois River and Nova Scotia. It wore a tattered cassock and dug for roots in the earth with Huron children. It learned to paddle, to live on berries and fish, and to speak various dialects of Iroquoian and Algonquian. This spirit lingered, in somber exile, telling its beads, making its rounds through snowy forests to preach the brotherhood of man to the tribes of the Ottawa and Niagara River valleys, the Great Lakes and the upper Ohio, muttering to the end the ancient prayers for holy martyrdom.

While disease and war decimated the Huron, a new spirit was busily staking its claims in the New World, mining silver with slave labor in the cloud forest at Potosí, building walled towns in the Virginia swamps and whitewashed churches at Albany. The modern world had arrived, and with it the Americans, and they had little use for either Huron or Jesuits.

Was it the vast dimensions of this tragedy that riveted Parkman all those years, the fascination afforded by an epic at once so pathetic, violent, and catastrophic? Throughout the books, Parkman lapses into frank admiration for the priests' and nuns' self-denial, and for the Huron's powers of endurance. But the essential natures of the participants were beyond the historian's comprehension. He must have perceived this as failure. His work and travels led to several breakdowns from nervous exhaustion. Constant study in bad light ruined his eyes. When his exhaustion threatened to overwhelm, he dismissed his assistants and worked in his garden.

The question punctuates the twenty-five hundred pages of the narrative: Who were these people? Who were they? Who were they? Over the course of a lifetime, he tracked their spirits, but in the end, they escaped him.

To be generous to the memory of the dead, both victor and vanquished; to preserve their stories in our classrooms and their pain in our hearts; to learn from them; to forgive the crimes of their age, as we hope our own crimes will be forgiven by posterity. An interesting and fallacious feature of the modern faith in progress is the conviction that we have become, through the ages and in significant ways, *better people*. Let history be the judge of that.

III

The name "Ohio" is derived from *Oyo*, or "great river" in Iroquoian. Like most places in the United States, the Ohio valley resembles a palimpsest and bears traces of a succession of peoples. Here the French preceded the first English settlers. The Shawnee and Miami and Huron arrived centuries before them. The people of the Adena and Hopewell cultures lived here thousands of years before the Shawnee and left giant mounds in the shape of serpents. The serpents remain, and they're visited throughout the year by schoolkids on field trips.

French is spoken along the Ohio again, no longer by voyageurs in canoes, but by Burundian and Tanzanian refugees, resettled by Catholic charities in Cincinnati. Many of the refugees are new congregants at the same parish my immigrant Irish granny belonged to when she arrived in this city to work in a silk-screening shop.

There's a German mass early Sunday mornings at Old Saint Mary's on Thirteenth Street, and a noon service in Swahili at Saint Leo the Great in Fairmount. Between these churches lies the Mill Creek industrial district, home to descendants of freed slaves who came north looking for work. Like most cities, it's a ferment, a patchwork, a low boil of immigration and dislocation, of new beginnings and last resorts, the unending human iterations of dispossession, resilience, and catch-as-catch-can.

That the past is condemned to be abandoned is a realization that comes, sooner or later, to most people. Some are not overly troubled by this; others are constitutionally afflicted with an inexpressible guilt at a failure that seems preordained and profoundly unjust. The latter see political blandishments to embrace the future as diversion and whitewash; they refuse to face the future before the sins of the past are properly tallied. They'll find little satisfaction, because the powers that be are accountable only to investors, and God knows there's no money in justice.

Perhaps this is for the best. The inability to forget would be a burden so crushing it would extinguish life in an instant. Selective memories have been selected for, written into our genetic code. In the process of completing the circle, and then erasing the circle altogether, it no longer occurs to most people to be grateful to the semi-oblivion in which they live and move.

But the desire to retain something persists, and some people are incapable of leaving anything behind. This dilemma can define a person, not always in salutary ways. Such people are overwhelmed by the obligation, compelling because unspoken, to forget nothing. But it's like carrying the world in a spoon.

When people speak of prophecy, they commonly think in terms of the future. But if you conceive of history as a threadbare tapestry, deteriorating and becoming less and less intelligible as you read backward through time, then the past begins to resemble, in its increasing obscurity, a mirror image of the future. Knowledge of the past extends but a few brief millennia, the present is mere flux, and tomorrow is a sheer blank. We are beset on three sides by darkness. It is a womb-like existence, absent the ready nourishment and the peace.

God took up the prophet in His hand and set him down in a valley of dry bones. "And he said unto me, Son of man, can these bones live? And I answered, O Lord God, thou knowest."[13] It was not, I think, to demonstrate His almighty powers that God set Ezekiel in that field of death.

God said to him, "Prophesy upon these bones, and say unto them, O ye dry bones, hear the word of the Lord."

It is the mortal, solitary, and insignificant human being who is instructed, and obliged, to bridge the gulf that separates the living and the dead. "So I prophesied as I was commanded: and as I prophesied, there was a noise, and behold a shaking, and the bones came together, bone to his bone." But words were not enough; there was no breath in the bones. "Then said he unto me, Prophesy unto the wind, prophesy, son of man, and say to the wind, Thus saith the Lord God; Come from the four winds, O breath, and breathe upon these slain, that they may live." If the people are ever to be healed and reconciled to their creator, the prophet had to wake the dead; wheresoever they are led, the people may not leave their past behind.

Christianity inherited this emphasis on remembrance, which was, in the words of historian Jacques Le Goff, "the mainspring of spiritual life" in the medieval Roman church. Le Goff, in *Saint Francis of Assisi*, points out that the "examination of conscience" is "primarily an act of remembering," which seems self-evident but is easily forgotten.[14] Virtue, for Francis, was grounded in unending recollection of the suffering of God and all God's creatures. The church's term for this remembrance—for the keeping of another's pain before one's eyes—is *recordatio*, with *cor* (heart) at its root.

If we fail to bring the past with us into the future, we will arrive less than human. A rootless and death-forgetting people have no one to forgive them, and nothing to forgive. They see no need for atonement, and therefore seek no absolution. For such a people, blameless in their own eyes, compassion and mercy become difficult.

"And if your brother becomes poor," reads Leviticus 25:35, "and falls into poverty among you; then you shall help him: yea, though he be a stranger, or a sojourner; that he may live with you." "Thou shalt neither vex a stranger," reads Exodus 22, "nor oppress him: for ye were strangers in the land of Egypt." In this sense, justice, without which there is no life, is founded in remembrance. A forgetful man becomes proud, sufficient unto himself. To preserve something of the past, no matter how revolting or ennobling, humanizes one.

If somebody had told me, as I sat at the kitchen table thirty-five years ago reading Parkman's book, that the dead were dead and that was that, I would have understood well enough what I was being told. But if the dead are dead, if the past is past, then the marketers and politicians are justified.

Lately, I'm troubled by an image, a waking nightmare of a nameless day in a nameless future. Two people, a woman and a man, are paddling down the Ohio in a small boat, past the relic factories and the brick depot buildings, past the toppled coal cranes and collapsed iron trestles; past the disused, overgrown, abandoned river towns. I wonder what they are thinking. They might be too consumed with more immediate concerns to speculate about the habits of a vanished people who left so much of the earth a waste and a ruin. If they think of us at all, it will be because they have no choice. Every bend of the river, as the pair drifts along, will reveal yet more discouraging evidence of our passage. Perhaps they will assign us a name, as people customarily do to their predecessors. Perhaps they will wish to forget about us, but it will not be possible.

IV

We arrived at the Wells Fargo bank tower one evening as the last office workers were departing. In the basement, five stories below the street, at the bottom of a long iron staircase, in the room where rumbling boilers the size of bull elephants drowned our voices, Derek shut off the water intake valve with a three-foot pipe wrench, then opened the relief. A stream of water the width of a stovepipe hammered the wall like a rock drill, and Derek leaned on the wrench and watched with equanimity as forty floors drained. By the time we reached the maintenance deck on the top floor, the tank that contained the building's water was empty.

The tank was the width of a garden shed and ten feet deep. Its iron walls were coated with a slick rusty film the color of Georgia clay, and the interior smelled like a disused mine. At the bottom of the tank was the occasion for all this business: a copper coupling with a small split, in size somewhat like an infected paper cut.

We worked through the night in a damp and discolored haze of scorched solder paste.

Quiet and hands-off, Derek had a talent for instruction not common among men. Turn the flame down, grasshopper, he told me as I knelt at the pipe with the acetylene torch. Keep a baby finger of blue heat on it. Let the flux draw. Touch the solder to the cup. Work around. Okay, kill it. Now let's see how bad you fucked things up.

At some miserable hour, we climbed out for a breath of air and stood at the window, high above the city. Bridge lights glittered on the black river. An ambulance drove down Fourth Street, its red light sweeping the brick facades like a research sub probing for life in a deep-sea canyon.

By five in the morning, the pipe was repaired, and Derek turned the water on again. By then my shirt was soaked and stiff with rust (Derek's not so much), and we walked out into the morning light and the traffic noise as into a dear and half-remembered world.

A year after I quit the plumbing job, I ran into Derek on Sixth Street as he was turning a corner with a bucket of tools. I had a new job as a bicycle messenger, and he regarded my helmet and pager with some amusement. Why not come back, he asked, and finish my apprenticeship? He would talk to the boss about getting me a little more money, he said. Another buck-fifty an hour maybe.

I was happy pedaling around town, I told him, I can't do that shit work anymore. When I said those words, he looked down the street as if he could see, past my shoulder, something unpleasant approaching, and I realized what I'd done. But it was too late to take the words back.

"Well, take care," he said. "Be in touch if you change your mind." He walked off, and that was the last time I saw him. I was too ashamed, and lacked the courage, to pick up the phone and apologize for the prideful and ugly thing I'd said to Derek, a man who had always been kind and generous to me, a man who, with patience and good humor, had taught me many useful things.

He died about a year after that day. He was not yet forty when he took his own life. I've dreamed of him since then. The tenor of the dreams is easy and warm, as when a friend drops by on a quiet afternoon, unexpectedly, for a coffee and a chat. The dreams become more vivid even as they become less frequent. The most recent dream takes place in a castle, high above the sea. Think of the opening scene, in the predawn fog and darkness—that hopeless hour of night—when Hamlet and the soldiers are awaiting the ghost. Imagine the same place, but in broad daylight, on a bright September afternoon, one of those mournful golden hours that graces the end of late summer days in higher latitudes, when time is a long expiration of light.

The place where we stand is open to the sky. Far below, the little ships rock gently, and their colorful pennants flutter in the breeze. There are people about, not for any special occasion, but simply to enjoy the beautiful weather. There are not many such days in Denmark, after all.

And there he is, leaning at the parapet, watching the water. "Derek," I say.

He straightens and smiles. "I'm not Derek." He is wearing the powder-blue company shirt and I point to the name patch above his breast pocket, where his own name is printed, and he laughs. "That's not me."

I don't understand, but it's not important. We watch the water together for a time. Then we shake hands and he walks away.

Between 1841 and 1842, cheated and robbed of their lands, the Huron were removed to Indian Territory. Harassment and theft attended the long migration, and cholera and hunger greeted them at their destination in Kansas. The tribe survived this trial, too, as well as the US government's assimilation and termination policies of the mid-twentieth century, and today numbers about five thousand members scattered across the United States. Many live in Wyandotte Nation in northeast Oklahoma.

Winter in the Capital

Mongolia, November

As we crest the ridge, the capital comes into view. Situated in a bowl of mountains, the city drowns in its own effluvium. Three smokestacks, rising to two hundred meters, pierce the settled smog like a disembodied battery of howitzers, the barrels dribbling smoke into the cobalt sky.

The bus begins the juddering descent down a switchback road, past pine groves that darken the snowy slopes like the shadows of clouds. The passengers are on the end of a two-day, six-hundred-mile drive across roadless central Mongolia in a Russian-built minibus, from Altai in the northwest Gobi (my Peace Corps post) to the capital, Ulaanbaatar. Bundled in traditional *deels* or in heavy coats, they peer in silence through frost-smeared windows.

The red clouds and blue sky of late afternoon give way to smog as the bus navigates the outskirts' cratered roads, past machine shops and ash-stained gers within cinder-block compounds. Figures bundled in thick coats hurry along the sagging walls, down the dirt lanes. Trash piles slump against the lee sides of buildings. Coal lies in heaps beside the ironmongers' stalls. Soon, the air inside the bus becomes a mix of burning trash, exhaust, and coal fires. The sky grows darker by touches.

The immense cooling towers of the power plants come into view, smoldering like a brace of volcanoes beside the frozen Tuul River. Sacred to Mongolians, the Tuul is desperately low these days, one of hundreds of dying rivers in this country. Trash studs the thin patches of ice.

Hundreds of feet high on a pole, the red, blue, and gold flag of

Mongolia hangs like a songbird from a limestick, a singular streak of color in an otherwise sterile afternoon whose sun appears as a bleary and intermittent stain. As the bus moves, the perimeter of visibility moves with it, closing in behind us while revealing more city ahead. The passengers wipe the windows with coat sleeves.

Over the next few days, a smell like scorched rime will seep into my clothes, and I'll carry the smell of the capital back to Altai and wear it on my coat till spring.

The imaginative faculty, Wordsworth believed, had atrophied in the bad air of industrialization, war, and economic dislocation. So many people, harassed and oppressed, had been spiritually and physically uprooted. His sister Dorothy's journals record the many beggars, homeless families, and demobbed soldiers who passed by the Wordsworths' cottage—the human reverberations of the continental wars, refugees adrift along the high roads.

The dream of a new world is an old dream. In his Revelation, John sees "a new heaven and a new earth, for the first heaven and the first earth had passed away."[1] This vision was embraced by the "Inner Light" movement of the Radical Reformers—Ranters, Seekers, Anabaptists, Friends of God—who thrived in seventeenth-century England and Holland. They sought to inaugurate the new earth in real time, here and now. In his *Mystery of God concerning the Whole Creation* (1648), Gerrard Winstanley, Leveller preacher and radical, promised that "the work of God shall finally be restored from its lost, dead, weedy, and enslaved condition."[2]

But the passion for intense and immediate communion with God and with creation had waned as the sects were persecuted and their members silenced, executed, or banished. Their star had set with the Puritans and Cromwell, well before Wordsworth's day, but echoes of that spirit lingered into the years of the poet's childhood. The north of England, where Wordsworth was born and raised and where he spent most of his life, was a center of much agitation and revivalism, as the

Quaker George Fox's memoirs testify. The names of the places where he preached read like a catalog of the poet's work. "From thence I passed through Northumberland to Derwentwater," Fox wrote in his journal,

> where there were great meetings . . . The next day we came into Cumberland again, where we had a general meeting of thousands of people . . . A great convincement there was in Cumberland, Bishoprick, Northumberland, Westmoreland, Lancashire, and Yorkshire; and the plants of God grew and flourished.[3]

Wordsworth and Coleridge planned to collaborate on a great work, one that would serve to check the growing despondency. It was their belief that poetry had the power to remove the scales from the eyes, allowing men and women to perceive the essential and underlying unity of life, the interdependence of all things, and humanity's blood relation with all creation.

> *Paradise, and groves*
> *Elysian, Fortunate Fields—like those of old*
> *Sought in the Atlantic Main, why should they be*
> *A history only of departed things,*
> *Or a mere fiction of what never was?*[4]

It would be a joyful enterprise, though nothing less than the soul of man was at stake. Humanity was subsiding into a spiritual torpor that could only issue in spiritual death. The philosophies and mental habits that had led to this crisis wanted correction. Such visions as the two poets shared, it seems, commonly thrive in times of political and economic turmoil.

Ulaanbaatar

That night, lying in a dorm bunk in a cramped and sour hostel, a cough and a fever prevent me from sleeping. I'm jangled by the weird energy of illness. My mind ranges as I search for my place in the book, to read again by flashlight the lines from the *Prelude*.

Witness—whatever falls my better mind,
Revolving with the accidents of life[5]

Wordsworth often composed at a late hour. His creative struggles are recorded in his sister's journals from their stay at Grasmere.

"Poor William," she calls him. "Dear William."[6]

Headaches, sleeplessness, and respiratory ailments plagued him. He suffered under the strain of his vision, under the "burden of the mystery" whose articulation nearly ruined his health.

Wordsworth believed that, by the free and loving exercise of their imagination, human beings were capable of creating the world anew—not figuratively, but truly. The poet did not espouse a return to Eden, but to a new earth that is precisely this earth, the quotidian miracle, the "produce of the common day." This new earth has been beside us all the while, he believed, but our eyes and ears can no longer perceive it, because our lives have become meager and bleak.

The imaginative act, ignited by empathy, is an act of sedition from received modes of perception. To see the humanity in human beings, and the beauty in the common day, was a rare gift in Wordsworth's day, no less than in ours. But poetry would dissolve the chains of tyrannizing habit, so often self-imposed; poetry would rinse the bleary panes of vision. For the poet, a wind-stunted tree possessed prophetic power, a daffodil was miraculous, a cloud lonely—and he wanted others to see these truths.

There is a strange story in Mark's Gospel that touches on this issue. In the district of Dalmanutha, people had gathered to hear the rabbi. As the crowd grew, the disciples fretted that they did not have enough bread to feed the people. The rabbi upbraided them, asking, "Why are you discussing the fact that you have no bread?" He attributed their misapprehension to a failure of nerve and, curiously, to a lack of compassion. "Do you not yet perceive or understand? Are your hearts hardened? Having eyes do you not see, and having ears do you not hear? And do you not remember?" The disciples, self-blinded, could not see with the eyes of the heart.

Medieval theologians had often lamented the passing of the Age of Miracles. Some claimed that vivid proofs of truth were no longer needed. Others claimed that a depraved humanity no longer deserved such demonstrations of God's love. Still others reached the conclusion that people no longer believed—and therefore could no longer *see*—that the touch of a hand could restore sight, or heal the sick, or make whole. For Wordsworth, however, the miraculous was as elemental as air, perceptible not to the privileged or to the educated, but to the open-hearted.

There are moments when eternity and time intersect. "Scenes different there are," Wordsworth writes in Book VII of *The Prelude*,

Full formed, which take, with small internal help,
Possession of the faculties . . .

The calmness, beauty of the spectacle,
Sky, stillness, moonshine, empty streets, and sounds
Unfrequent as in desarts[7]

These moments reveal themselves "when no one looks about, / Nothing is listened to," when you finally give audience to the voice of the One who has waited so long, and so patiently, to be heard.

The Revolution in France had been a source of hope for English radicals such as Wordsworth and Coleridge, and its failure was demoralizing. In the years following the Terror, as Napoleon's armies ravaged the continent, life in England was marked by increased repression and unrest. Coleridge subsided into opiate addiction, an unhappy marriage, and a crippling lack of confidence. The period of 1805 to 1814—corresponding to the meridian and decline of Napoleon's fortunes and the near-constant fear of invasion in England—was also marked by intense personal grief for the Wordsworths. Their brother John died in February 1805 (the year

William finished *The Prelude*, arguably his greatest work, which would remain unpublished during his lifetime); William's first break with his dear friend Coleridge occurred in 1810; and his daughter Catherine and son Thomas both died in 1812. Long gone were the days of revolutionary promise, when young idealists believed that a new dawn of universal peace and liberty was soon to break out in the world, when "to be young was very heaven," as the poet said. His sister Dorothy, too, grew increasingly unwell.

In 1814, Wordsworth composed *The Excursion*, which was intended to serve as the first part of an epic envisioned as a "Gothic cathedral" built of philosophic verse. The cathedral was never built; the project was abandoned. Coleridge drifted into German metaphysics and organic philosophy, while Wordsworth traded his youthful idealism for orthodox religion and a government job. Keats's letters reveal a pompous, disdainful old man, but the young poet found the generosity to forgive Wordsworth's arrogance by recalling his ability to "think into the human heart."[8]

The unitive vision is the perennial dream of poets, and the eternal delusion of mystics. It is a yearning for a return to Eden, wherever that might be, where everything is preordained, where the torment of choice is unknown. It is a sad vision, known above all to lonely men and women.

Wordsworth never discarded his faith in the power of the imagination to reveal a presiding spirit at work in the universe, a spirit in which every leaf and mountain and human being participates. I don't know if the poet read Thomas à Kempis, but he would have shared the canon's belief that "if thy heart were right, then every creature would be a mirror of life and a book of holy doctrine."[9] Despite a lifetime of personal tragedy and professional disappointment, cruel reviews and the loss of friends, Wordsworth never relinquished his belief in the truth of this vision.

Late in the night, I come across some lines in which the poet writes of the moon, his love for which he likens to his love for country, which is a damn silly notion. I mistrust Wordsworth when he writes as a Christian or a patriot, but I would not condemn such a thing. As when a good friend tells you something that you know is only half true, and you both look away for a moment, but you do not criticize them because you love them, and because they have forgiven the same fault in you many times.

Snow lashes the deserted square, 3:00 a.m., and I think of my family. My dad almost never spoke of God or religion. In his opinion, if you were a man who assumed as his role in life the right to dictate the thoughts and actions of other men; that is, if you were a man who claimed to know the Truth, and took it upon yourself to share your wisdom for the edification of those around you; that is to say, if you were an evangelist or a politician (and it's a fact that most men moonlight as priests and politicians)—well, you were probably an asshole. His philosophy, theology, and religion could be summed up in two questions: "Really? And who the hell are you?" Being a quiet man, he did not say this in so many words. But a kid learns to interpret things.

It must have been the cold—a night frost laced with smoke—that made me think of the bar my parents owned. On school days, my dad woke my brother and me at 4:00 a.m. to go clean the place. At that hour, the bar smelled of spilled draft beer and cigarettes. On the wooden tables, tin ashtrays lay buried under heaps of butts. We gathered the plastic cups and paper plates, swept pretzel crumbs onto the wooden floor planks. It was my task to take the trash out behind the bar to a perforated metal can and burn it, stirring the Styrofoam-and-paper-plate fire with a wooden paling as I stood in the snow and blew into my fists. I enjoyed burning the trash. My dad and brother were probably content to let me have that particular job. It didn't occur to me then that a person would voluntarily pass on the chance to burn things.

Mop the floors; fill the coolers; wipe the bar; restock the snack racks with thirty-cent sacks of Husman pretzels and corn chips. The place opened early. Saint James Elementary School was across the street, and I went to class smelling, so I was informed, of burnt plastic.

One morning, as I swept beneath the stools, I found a wad of dollar bills. I smoothed them and counted thirteen, and I put the bills in my pocket. For an hour I went through my chores, agonizing on the horns of a dilemma. Thirteen dollars to a nine-year-old boy in 1978 could buy a model kit of a German Panther tank and two half-pound Hershey chocolate bars. I knew the money belonged to someone else, and if I told my dad he would make a few calls and the money would be lost to me forever, along with the chocolate. So I put it off until I couldn't justify the thing any more. I found my dad standing inside a narrow closet, arranging items on a shelf. I told him I'd found some money, and I pulled out the cash to show him.

"Keep it," he said. He didn't even look at my hand.

In his late forties and early fifties, Wordsworth wrote the *Ecclesiastical Sonnets*, a verse history of religion in England from the Druids to the poet's day. Of Wordsworth's poetry, it is presently little read and less esteemed. By 1822, when the *Sonnets* were published, Wordsworth was past fifty and deeply acquainted with loss. "We are not destroyed by death," wrote Saint Paul. I wonder what Wordsworth thought of those words.

To the end of his life, he never disavowed the existence of some spirit, some genius of desolation or of pity that, while untouched by the works and days of women and men, was nevertheless, in some small way, mindful of them. Here is an excerpt from those *Sonnets*:

Truth fails not; but her outward forms that bear
The longest date do melt like frosty rime,
That in the morning whitened hill and plain
And is no more; drop like the tower sublime
Of yesterday, which royally did wear
His crown of weeds, but could not even sustain
Some casual shout that broke the silent air,
Or the unimaginable touch of Time.[10]

Around me in the dark, bodies cough and wheeze and shift heavily in the bunks. Sleepless, racked with a wrenching cough, I am lucid, feverish, past reason. I close the book. Winter air whistles through the rattly sashes, and the words ring.

Spring Arrives in the Gobi

the wind before the rain,
the crow before the wolf

—PROVERB

Altai, Mongolia

Some winters are so cold, they say, a young bull's horns will crack. On certain sunny and windless days in January, when the temperature rises to negative twenty degrees at noon and the light is pure and powder-dry, tiny crystals of ice glint in the air, a spangling of color delicate as surf spray. I don't know where the crystals come from, whether swept up on a breeze too light to feel, or carried down from the mountains on the wind. Waterfalls create reflection rainbows; icy breezes stir "diamond dust": iridescence, or irisation in various iterations. Coleridge, in a late poem, called it simply "the gemmy air."

There's a Mongolian word for this display. I once heard a man use it and asked him to repeat it for me. I neglected to write down the word, and when I went home, I could no longer recollect what I'd heard. Forgetting my notebook that day was an act of carelessness. I must learn to pay attention.

One day near the end of winter, I departed from my usual circuit of primary schools and carried my Mongol-English grammars and my plastic sack of chalk to the technical college outside of town, where I was scheduled to assist the English instructor. On the way through the ger district, I passed a pile of tires burning in an intersection. The streets of frozen mud were deserted, and the fire burned unattended. Smoke from wood and dung and coal fires rose from the ivory-colored tents while vigilant and weather-bitten dogs, chained or loose, patrolled the fences of every compound. The oily flames of the tire fire afforded the only color in a gray landscape of weathered palings and low clouds.

The students, seventeen- and eighteen-year-old seamstresses, sat quietly in wooden chairs, bundled in heavy coats, subdued and weary-seeming in the cold dim room. Before setting off for school, they would have fetched water, prepared milk tea for younger siblings, finished their homework. It often falls to the oldest girl in the family to start the fire to heat the ger in the morning. When they wake before dawn to light the dung or raw coal, the temperature inside will have fallen into the thirties. The ger might be home to three generations: the student's younger sibling or siblings, a mother, often a father, a grandparent or two, perhaps an uncle suffering from an injury or a drinking problem.

The teacher, who spoke little English, passed around xerox copies of a page from an instruction manual that must have dated from the 1950s. Sewing terminology in English constituted the hour's lessons, and the young women recited the words *spindle* and *bobbin* and *treadle*.

There is no textile industry in Altai, and few jobs of this sort in the capital. The closest these students will come to careers as seamstresses will probably be in a South Korean sweatshop. Recent graduates, I would wager, are doing exactly that as I write this, sending money home to their families. How many of the students wonder, as they sit taking notes, where they will be in a year, or in five years? Perhaps some of them harbor a secret faith in their stars or in the lama's prognostications that the future holds something worthwhile for them, something besides early pregnancy, an abusive husband, or servitude to poor relations. But the modern world will squander their trust and talents, their tremendous resources of self-discipline. Those ghostly old words, *spindle* and *bobbin*, rang in my ears for days.

Spring officially arrives with the second new moon of the calendar year, usually in early February. Tsagaan Sar, or the White Moon festival, is the most important event in the Mongolian calendar. The people of the town prepare by cleaning their apartments and gers, and by cooking dumplings, thousands of them for each household. In the streets, children scrub and beat carpets. Winter coats and bedding are washed and hung to dry in the freezing sunshine. On the day of the new moon, the people wake before dawn, dress in traditional deels, greet one another with handshakes and formal kisses, and exchange gifts. Grandmothers and wives make libations of milk to the sky.

Students and teachers and staff arrive at school before first light. Spectral figures in blue and silver and rose-colored robes, laughing and chatting, hurry toward the doors in the bitter dark. It is a grueling time of year, and the cleaning, cooking, drinking, and visiting may last up to a month. In the latter days of the festival, the teachers are bleary with exhaustion and will lay their heads on their desks and sleep while I take over their lessons.

A few weeks after the White Moon festival, the black kites return, harbingers of the annual dust storms. The winds pound on the wooden walls of the apartment building. Telephone wires belly and rock, and the day turns burnt yellow with howling gusts of sand. Many Mongolians hate the wind. It causes eye infections among livestock. It puts a person on edge. A storm might last for hours, as yellow sheets of trash and dust lash the empty streets.

By March, when the winds are fiercest, the produce at the shops will have grown scanter but, for the townspeople at any rate, there are usually potatoes and carrots to be had, and perhaps a jar of tomato preserves from Poland. Mutton and horsemeat are reliable options. Conditions in the countryside, however, will be more precarious. As winter turns to spring, hunger often visits the nomads husbanding their flocks on the steppe. They must care for sick animals, feed their children, contend with wolves and snow. In front of School #3, mornings at 8:00 a.m., taxis bring the herders' children to school. Some of the taxi drivers ferry the children over the mountains on motorcycles and arrive wearing scarves across their faces like stick-up men, their eyes livid and ice-fringed. The little girls and boys in thick coats clamber off the backs of the bikes and run for the doors. Their red cheeks, iconic from *National Geographic* photo essays of Tibet or Ladakh, are symptomatic of incipient frostbite.

The students love school. Temperatures dipping to negative thirty degrees do not discourage them. They love meeting their friends and teachers each morning, and they greet the foreigner with shouts of *uglu-unii mend, bagsh aa*. Good morning, my teacher.

You can read the hard weather on the faces of the herdsmen when they visit town for supplies. They ride motorcycles over miles of snow-covered steppe, dressed in broad-belted woolen cloaks. Their expressions, as they wander the town, are half-contemptuous, half-disbelieving, as if they've debarked on a planet they instinctively dislike. The presence of a foreigner seems a mild insult to some nomads, and others are frankly bewildered by the stranger's face. Generally, however, they are too preoccupied with the demands of survival to bother with such trivialities. They get what they need and go.

As the days lengthen, more birds return. A friend from one of the eastern provinces called to say she had spotted a hoopoe, and the next day I saw one myself: a crow-sized, cinnamon-colored bird with a long, curved beak and a spotted crest, a beautiful flyer displaying a black-and-white wing pattern in flight. A pair of pied wheatears, like miniature magpies, appeared one morning on a stone fence.

On a March weekend, I rode along with a teacher's family to their village, located some two hundred miles from Altai, to visit the teacher's parents and siblings. Suvd, her husband Nergui, their young daughter, and I rode in a compact car for twelve hours over dirt tracks that, in places, had been effaced by wind and rain. We bogged down twice in the sand and twice dug our way out. There were no vehicles to be seen, so we stopped often to scan the steppe, trying to spy the best way forward. Halfway there, we spread a blanket on the sand and ate cold noodles and mutton, oranges and chocolate, and shared a can of beer.

Sand devils patrolled the distances, and mountains shaped the compass of the horizon. The emptiness was relieved, after several more hours of travel, by a man leading a file of shaggy bronze camels toward town. The town of Khokhmorit, or Blue Horse, is situated at the base of the Mongol Sands, a chain of towering dunes stretching for two hundred fifty miles across the northwest Gobi. Beyond the town, beyond the dunes, snowy peaks hover in the middle air like a grim palace locked in perennial winter.

At the entrance to the village is an *ovoo*, a cairn of stones festooned with sky-blue scarves for luck. Empty vodka bottles and small-denomination bills are tucked between the stones. Near the ovoo is a blue-painted, concrete statue of a horse, and beneath the statue's belly we find a raven's nest. The raven circles, bawling at the intrusion. Her nest is lined with soft gray feathers, but it's too early in the year for eggs or nestlings. Suvd's aged mother, having come with great effort to the edge of town to welcome her daughter's family, pours spoonfuls of milk onto each of the little car's four worn and dusty tires, in observance of their faithful service.

Suvd's father is frail and unwell, but he greets me warmly with a proffered snuff bottle. He wears the wispy moustache and stained fedora of a disreputable Chinese poet. The family laughs continually at his comments, made at my expense, for friendly harassment is a sign of affection. In-laws drop by to greet the arrivals. It's been months since they've seen one another. A bowl of vodka makes the rounds. Mother serves *tsuivan*, noodles with fatty mutton, and I sleep comfortably, along with the grandchildren, in a blanket on the floor, my face warmed by the dung fire rumbling in the stove.

By April, the cold doesn't burn anymore, and if you stand still long enough, very still, and close your eyes, you can feel the warmth of the sun settle light as a breath on your face. The piercing clarity of the sunlight, as the days pass, loses its edge.

One day, I watched a bird circle the steppe, too large to be a kite. It lighted on a far ridge, a hunched black shape pacing the crest. If I had not seen it drop from the sky, I would have assumed it to be an old hermit draped in a black cloak, lost on the windy moors, involved in dark thoughts. When the bird spread its cloak and took flight, I saw that it was a vulture, a lammergeier. Ossifrage in Latin: bone-eater.

The mountains gleamed with snow. I heard the chipping of small birds around me. Although I stopped several times and stood still and listened, I could not locate them.

More birds returned every day. In the hills outside of town, Mongolian larks reclaimed their homes among the scattered stones. Mornings, at first light, I'm awakened by house sparrows stropping their beaks on my window sill.

Beside the resident pigeons, only crows and ravens overwinter here, as far as I can tell. They survive on the frozen carcasses of sheep and goats dumped at the edge of town. On the steppe in winter, there are only three colors: the blue sky, the white earth, and the black ravens. The steppe would be lonelier without them.

The land turned brown as the snow melted, then acquired a dusting of green. More like a suggestion, a hint of green, like the skin of a kiwi. While I wasn't looking, the land changed, and in one day suspicion turned to fact. Spring has a way of arriving unannounced. The date of the equinox is fixed on the calendar and people set their clocks forward and they know the change is coming, but the actual transition, nevertheless, surprises. Awareness of spring's arrival comes with a mild jolt, the way your shadow greets you after several sunless days. You look, and look again, and sense that something is not the same.

Dorothy Wordsworth remarked this gentle sleight of the season: "We sate in the orchard after dinner—it was a beautiful afternoon. The sun shone upon the level fields, and they grew greener beneath the eye."[1]

The grass grew in brief scattered patches beneath my feet, but the overall effect, as I looked out, was of new life. There were now white and yellow, blue and red flowers among the tufts of new grass.

I brought a copy of the *Georgics* on a walk to the mountain.

It was springtime then, great spring
Enhanced the earth and spared it the bitter breath of an east wind—
A time when the first cattle lapped up the light, and men

Children of earth themselves arose from the raw champaign,
And wild things issued forth in the wood, and stars in the sky.
How could so delicate creatures endure the toil they must,
unless between cold and heat there came this temperate spell
And heaven held the earth in his arms and comforted her?[2]

In a shallow ditch, a dead dog swarmed with flies. It was asserted by medieval thinkers that flies did not need to enter Noah's ark because they were spontaneously generated by rotting carcasses. They had this from Virgil, and Virgil had it from another place. The old knowledge has a way of revealing more about humanity than about nature; for instance, the way a bundle of old clothing will generate a mouse. These notions, so unsophisticated to nowaday ears, will always be dearer to me, in a way, than fact.

Flight fast and agile, graceful with shallow beats; soars on flat wings with tail fanned and commonly hovers into wind. When breeding noisy—typically silent at other times. (*Birds of East Asia*)[3]

Kestrels have a curious habit. They will pace a person who is walking along a fence or beneath telephone lines. One spring in New Mexico, as I walked to school each day, I became acquainted with an American kestrel that perched every morning on the powerline above the road. When I came within twenty steps, she set off and perched again farther on. By relays, in this manner, she paced me for a mile to an intersection, where she broke off and headed for the waste ground between some apartment buildings. The bird did this several days in a row.

Today outside of Altai, perched on a fence, a familiar sight greets me: the short and curved beak, the wingtips reaching past the root of the tail, the smooth and dark-gray head and rufous shoulders: Kestrel, Eurasian male. When I am about twenty paces off, he flies farther down the fence line, re-alights on the wire, and waits again. We repeat this for over a mile before he veers into the open steppe.

I see him, out in the middle distance, hovering in the breeze, drawn to movement in the sparse grass. His wings flutter above his fixed and down-turned head, as though he is looking over the edge of himself. Like a butterfly on a string, he appears—or a Byzantine silversmith's costliest piece: a delicate mechanism of fins and springs, wound-up tight and tense with life.

The guide notes that the American kestrel is a vagrant from this part of Asia, and I think of my acquaintance in New Mexico, the female whose forebears had, like people, carried their curious habits to far-off continents. There's a term from ornithology, *vagility*, which refers to a species' ability to roam, to wander, to adapt to new elements, to settle new grounds. It's an unevenly distributed talent, I suspect, among kestrels no less than among humans.

A cloud passes across the sun and acquires a vibrant fringe of greens, blues, and reds. Irisation is a function of altitude, barometric pressure, high-desert aridity, time of day. *Function* was the word that first occurred to me, and I'll keep it there. But I wonder why I think of this display in terms of a function. To my mind, trained to see the world in the usual ways, natural phenomena are mediated by natural forces. There is a reason for the rainbow color in the clouds, as there is for everything that pertains to sensory experience. To the ancient or medieval mind, innocent of meteorology, this light might have been perceived as merely manifest, an uncreated thing, both mysterious and proper.

Over the past three hundred years, people have learned much about the universe, but human nature remains fixed. This will change. The visionary discoveries of the future will not be about the solar system but about ourselves, and they will be more difficult to believe in than continental drift once was, or heliocentrism. The Copernican theories will be mere thought exercises compared to the reckonings to come. No tools will be required by the future discoverer, no telescopes or star charts. Just a quiet spot, and time to think. Copernicus himself, it is said, rarely looked at the night sky.

Samuel Taylor Coleridge was haunted by visions he feared to name. His daughter, Sara Coleridge, was a writer and a scholar. She edited her father's works and came to understand his failures through his writings. "Whatever subject I commence," she wrote, describing both herself and the poet, "I feel discontent unless I could pursue it in every direction to the farthest bounds of thought, and then, when some scheme is to be executed, my energies are paralyzed with the very notion of the indefinite vastness which I long to fill."[4] Her confession makes me wonder at the extent to which the boundaries that define our ignorance are set by natural intellectual limitations, which we may not transcend, or by fear, which we might.

Copernicus would have understood her. His great work, *On the Revolutions of the Heavenly Bodies*, the culmination of a lifetime of labor, was offered to his pupil Rheticus after years of misgiving and hesitation, and it was printed only after the astronomer's death.

The visionaries of science and art, those who have revealed the most troublesome things about our world, have often died brokenhearted and misunderstood, penniless and disregarded, consumed with self-doubt and remorse. That's not ironic, but just as it ought to be, given what little I know about myself. The one who, some day soon, steps forward to reveal humankind to itself will no doubt have much cause to regret her trouble.

Fire-colored clouds barrel down the mountains, dragging rain. *Shoroo shuurag* in Mongolian: earth storm. The slack powerlines rock over the dirt roads. Trash and dust stream in channels along the ground, down every east-running lane.

Three schoolboys dressed in blue polyester jackets squint behind a wooden fence with their mouths buried in the crooks of their elbows. From a tall brick stack at the coal plant, a tassel of black smoke trails the ground. The wind growls at the window sash; sheet metal clatters on the roof. I put on a hat and walk out. The mountains are just visible, a chain of enchanted islands above the layer of haze that cinches the horizon. The sky is a shifting patchwork of dust and rain. A cloud immanent with watery light towers over the ger district and casts the weathered tents into shadow.

The dogs of the Big Pack—my name for the town's resident band of strays—are curled up asleep in the dust of a coal shed. Not one of them stirs. Only people are about, hurrying from wall to wall. These winds will sweep across northern China and sift toxic dust over Tokyo and Seoul, and meteorologists in California will soon detect pollutants from Beijing in the air over Humboldt County.

—

> You have learned why winter fetters the earth, and spring sets it free, why the summer is hot, why autumn is the season of harvest; why Boreas is chill and Favonius mild; why the one lays waste the flowers, while the other adorns the earth. . . . I have taught the winds to spread abroad the vessels of rain, that showers of moisture may reagglomerate earth that has disintegrated into sterile dust . . . (*Cosmographia*, Bernardus Silvestris, 12 CE)[5]

"Not the whole earth was given for the wind to range over." There are tranquil places, too. Each of the sons of Eos "has his home," according to Ovid, and yet

> *So wildly the brothers quarrel, even now*
> *The world is almost torn in a war of winds.*[6]

Boreas of the "wind-tanned cheeks" lives in a cave in the uncharted north. It was Boreas who rocked free the beached Greek ships at war's end, enabling them to launch for home. He "spoke aloud in fluttering sails and hawsers" and led the captive-laden fleet away from the burning city. Perhaps he was complicit, too, in Poseidon's ruse, playing the double agent, lulling the Greeks into a false sense of security, spreading the lie that their ordeal had come to an end when, in fact, for so many, it was only beginning. In his turn, Boreas is subject to a higher power, King Aeolus, who rules

> *the contending winds and moaning gales*

As warden of their prison. Round the walls
They chafe and bluster underground. The din
Makes a great mountain murmur overhead.
High on a citadel enthroned,
Scepter in hand, he mollifies their fury,
Else they might flay the sea and sweep away
Land masses and deep sky through empty air.[7]

Down to the days of sailing ships, the notion persisted that the North Wind came from a fixed place on earth, and if a ship were to sail far enough northward, it would eventually reach the blind side of the wind's home, a place they called Hyperborea, a temperate region known (on the testimony of the poets) to be perennially sunny and calm. In his work "On Learned Ignorance," Nicolas of Cusa (d. 1464) lamented that there were still to be found "fools and men without wit and judgment who believe," among other absurdities, that the northernmost seas are completely frozen over.[8]

This belief arose in part from the conviction, peculiar to Judeo-Christian thought, that there simply must be a beginning and an end to things. "I have already described my ideas concerning this hemisphere and its form," Columbus asserted to his patrons, "and I have no doubt, that if I could pass below the equinoctial line . . . I should find the earthly paradise, whither no one can go but by God's permission."[9]

How many had their hopes cruelly disappointed during those early northern voyages, when they found not sunny calm, but a desolation of ice and darkness they could not believe?

At four in the morning, a breathtaking stillness wakes me. An eye of pale light on the pane is the reflection of the candle flame. A light rain, the first of the year, drips on the sill. I open the window to admit the moldy, iron smell of earth, and the silence.

Little rain has fallen in recent years, and the rivers, as they vanish, are giving up their secrets. One spring morning, wandering a riverbed, I find a metal pail, an empty bottle of Chinggis vodka, a red plastic boot. A motorcycle's gas tank, a goat carcass.

A ram's horn, too.

After he slew the boar, Theseus turned his back on worldly troubles for a spell and set out on a journey. When he came to the river Achelous, he found it a raging and impassable flood, so Achelous kindly advised Theseus to rest awhile. The god remarked indifferently on the angry waves wreaking havoc in the fields all around, as though the floodwaters were someone else's mischief and not his own.

Theseus entered the god's habitation and there he found other friendly travelers, among them Ixion's son and a few veterans of Troy, enjoying food and drink in plenty. Achelous charmed them with the story of his life, how he "swelled with anger and grew big with flood" one year when a feast was held for the local gods. You see, the river folk had neglected to invite Achelous to the feast. They would not make that mistake twice.

While his visitors enjoyed the river's generosity, Achelous told them of the girl he once loved, whose father killed her, and whom Achelous, in his grief, turned into an island. He spoke of his famed combat with Hercules, not without shame. The brute had ripped the horn from Achelous's head, and the scar was still visible on his brow. When the girls who performed the sacred rites to the river found this horn, they filled it with "gay fruits and sweet flowers" and gave it to Demeter, who now carries it, spillingly, over the fields at harvest time.

Achelous spoke with reluctance of his life's disappointments. "Which one of us likes to talk about his failures?" Scars, he tells the travelers, are reminders of loss and sorrow.

Something compelled Achelous to share his bitterest memories with his visitors. It was the price of hospitality, I suppose, and his guests listened with grave attention to the stories. Perhaps the river's pain found its reflection in memories of their own defeats, unrequited loves, and missed chances.

When the flood subsided, Ovid writes, the visitors gathered kit and resumed their separate journeys,

and as they left him, native Achelous

Concealed his weatherbeaten face, his wound, his scars
Beneath the surface of the rising waves.[10]

I come to a streambed choked with tumbleweeds. The tumbleweeds of the Gobi are different than those which wander the Chihuahuan Desert in the American Southwest. A tumbleweed in Texas's Big Bend is large, sometimes the size of a medicine ball. Imagine an outsize Leyden jar of brown electric light.

The Big Bend tumbleweed is "full," so to speak. The component twigs reach into the center and range throughout the form. The Gobi tumbleweed is much smaller, and empty. The component twigs are superficial. It resembles a desiccated globe on which all the river systems of the world are etched as with a steel pen, more fantastically than accurately but no less true for all that. If you hold a Gobi tumbleweed in your hand, then set it down, it leaves many tiny thorns in your palm, translucent as kitten teeth. In a ditch, I find dozens of them of various sizes, finished products of the globe-master's shop, works intended for no buyer but set free to the lunatic wind. Miracles of craftsmanship, they have traveled many desert miles.

The wind has brushed the horizon with a band of pink dust. Bottles lie broken on the ground like shattered brown and blue puddles, each shard reflecting the bright, high-desert light. Sheep bones and skulls lie in profuse heaps beside the streambed.

nor slept the winds
Within their stony caves, but rush'd abroad
From the four hinges of the world, and fell
On the vext Wilderness
(Paradise Regained, Book IV)[11]

The wind is bottomless—part maddening, part nauseating—a good sort of sickness. On the rising slopes beneath the mountain ridge, the land is stripped by wind to bare stones.

The old religions were born in bare and windy places, too. Born severe, tenacious as tamarisk or cactus. They hold a rattler's fascination for these reasons.

The old desert religions will surely be destroyed, worn to bones by the wind that neither forgets nor remembers. Then another religion will arise in another desert, and it will wear the bones of the dead faiths on strings, as anklets and necklaces, because they are beautiful. The new religion will speak to us familiarly, will beckon us to the top of a mountain, where it will seem strange to find ourselves, as in long-ago days, face to face once more.

On an aimless walk, I saw a bird perched on a heap of stones. It was unfamiliar to me so I sketched its likeness in an end page of a paperback. When I returned home and thought to check my sketch against the photographs in the bird guide, I found that the sketch resembled nothing so much as a butcher's diagram.

Many weeks earlier, in late February, I saw a solitary vulture kiting above the abandoned factory, and I took it for a sign of warmer days. But it disappeared, the cold and snow returned, and I didn't see another vulture for months. Perhaps that bird had been on reconnaissance. It had come scouting and found the taste of the air not to its liking, and so it had returned to India, where its cousins were living richly off the refuse heaps of Mumbai, awaiting auspicious breezes.

But on this April morning, as I walk toward snow-covered Khantaishir, I see nine vultures roosting on open ground, all facing the wind, ill-concealed by a few strands of brown grass. They have returned to stay, and a good time it is for them, for many animals perished during the long Mongol winter and their carcasses would be thawing on a day like this, sunny and forty degrees.

The vultures lumber into the air, sturdy kiters in ragged formation. They adjust incrementally to the angle of wind, with a dip of the wing or a brief tilt of the tail fan. I like to think the old sailors studied vultures when they were learning the improbable art of tacking into the wind, a skill that carried them across oceans.

The dogs of the Big Pack, ten or twelve of them, have come out of the town to feed on the carcasses of sheep and goats. Not the emaciated pariahs of south Asian cities, these strays are large Tibetan mastiffs, lively dogs with rich, dark coats. All year they roam the streets of Altai and the surrounding plains at will, a raucous gang of thieves, tongues lolling, trotting shoulder to shoulder as they make the rounds. As often as not, they appear to be on a purposeless jaunt. It's not pleasant to encounter the Big Pack at night, but I feel glad when I see them in the light of day. They exude a hilarious freedom. On the streets at noon, they shame the dour men in business suits and uniforms. They're beautiful dogs.

Now they're running toward something I can't see, far out on the steppe. They don't give a damn. They give no thought to tomorrow (knowing tomorrow is sufficient to the evil thereof) and neither do they store up their grain in barns. They race for the skyline, kicking up snow.

After an eight-mile hike I reach the crest of Khantaishir. On the other side is a wilderness of ridges separated by steep, cool, V-shaped valleys cloaked in brown needleleaf forest. The mountains roll and break against the far horizon. Nearly two years have passed since I first hiked up here: it is the same and not the same.

There are snow leopards in this province, I'm told, though others say it's not so. A book of Mongolian biota states that there are, but precariously few. Perhaps, I thought, somewhere in those mountain forests, a snow leopard is right now on the move, trailed by a few cubs that are no longer cubs. I wonder how they fared during the long winter.

There is little expectation of seeing a snow leopard, a fact which projects my hopes and fears in an irrational light and confirms the paradox that we most dread and desire what's most unlikely. When I am in my right mind, I wish only for snow leopards, in these mountains, for all time. I don't care if I ever see one. Call it the grizzly bear effect (or maybe an exotic strain of Stockholm syndrome, if you really think about it). But if a scientist were to announce tomorrow that snow leopards have vanished forever from the western Gobi, I will never forgive myself.

That afternoon, on the long walk down from Khantaishir, my mind wandered unaccountably to books I hadn't read for many years: Nordhoff and Hall's trilogy about Captain Bligh and the *Bounty* mutiny. Perhaps the endless wind suggested something of the sea.

Bligh and a few loyal officers, the story goes, are forced by the mutineers into an open boat. Granted a few scant provisions, they begin the long voyage to the nearest port, some thousands of miles across the South Pacific. The mutineers assumed that Bligh would never be heard from again, would never survive to accuse or to testify. For this reason, and as a bribe to guilty consciences, they gave Bligh and his officers a sporting chance in the form of a few primitive navigation devices. The mutineers lived to regret this small clemency.

After a number of days, suffering the first stages of exposure, Bligh's lieutenant begins to hallucinate. "The sea is so vast and so quiet," the man says, "I begin to doubt its reality and our own as well."

Bligh is amused by the remark. "That's a strange notion, sir," he says. "But the sea is real enough. I can promise you that."[12]

Largely by dead reckoning—by sun and stars—Bligh proceeded to guide the boat across six thousand miles of open sea to the Dutch port of Batavia in present-day Indonesia, arguably the greatest recorded navigational feat in the history of Western sail.

Faith is irrational, difficult, lonely. But to affirm only that which can be verified by the senses is to live by bread alone, which, as the rabbi knew, nourishes flesh not spirit.

Whether to live by bread alone, or by insubstantial visions of the mountain's far side, and the white leopards that wander there. God, like the snow leopard, is a nagging suspicion, a specter on the blind slope of a ridge, a starved mountain cat nosing through ground clutter for chipmunks.

A few miles from town, I heard a rifle shot and turned to see a dog run, yelping, for a short distance, then pitch into the ground. Its head lifted once and fell back, and then it grew still. A white, Russian-built, open-bed truck with tinted windows drove toward the dog. The rifleman, the dog, and I were the only bodies within sight in all that enormous land. I could see enough of the rifleman to know he'd been drinking, and I walked past at a distance, as unobtrusively as I could, willing myself small.

When the truck passed me, I saw dead dogs stacked in the bed—the dogs of the Big Pack. I knew them by their rich black fur. As the truck jounced over the rough ground, the dogs' bodies rolled in a massy heap, in the manner of warm meat. Further on, the truck halted and the rifleman squatted at the tailgate and defecated in a patch of snow.

It's real enough. I can promise you that.

A Natural History of New Mexico

I. State Highways

Night vision frays over time. When driving in darkness, I lean in to peer through the windshield, keep both hands on the wheel. On New Mexico's western plateau, past midnight, my vision is continually confounded by points of light—headlights, tail lights, transmission tower beacons—arrayed in shifting patterns across a hundred square miles of desert.

The mind drifts along the sweeping turns. Beyond the passenger window, a swatch of stars is blotted, not by a cloud, but by the sudden soaring wing of a mesa that emerges prow-first from the earth like a dreadnought breaching the surface after many sunken years.

The running lights of tractor trailers, miles ahead, dip and rise and swerve, and sometimes, to my disconcertment, disappear altogether.

A refinery glides past like a cruise liner trimmed stem to stern in strands of gold lighting, oppressively festive. The afterimage smolders behind my eyes for miles.

II. Society & People

Mr. O'Meara is tormenting the athletes.

On this Friday afternoon, the van carries eight passengers for the two-hour drive from Gallup to Albuquerque, where the state competition is to commence the next morning. Mr. O'Meara and his wife, Jeanne, have volunteered for Special Olympics New Mexico for twenty-five years. For decades, as specialists and teachers' aides and volunteers, they've worked with kids with exceptionalities.

Sarah, seated behind the driver, is an athlete, a distance walker. She announces to the passengers that we will arrive at the hotel in Albuquerque at "seven o'clock sharp." That was a mistake.

"I'm afraid not, Sarah," says Mr. O'Meara.

Sarah's face darkens. "Why not, Mr. O'Meara? Don't play games with me. Why not?"

"Didn't you hear the news? Nine Eight Seven."

"What?"

"There is no seven anymore. Nine ate seven."

"I'm warning you, Mr. O'Meara. Don't do this."

"Sarah, please don't shout. Your voice," says Jeanne, touching her forehead. "It's just. Really. Loud."

"Terrible shame," Mr. O'Meara says, "how nine ate seven."

Sarah is livid. She glares at Mr. O'Meara over the frames of her glasses.

"Just ignore him, Sarah," Jeanne pleads. "It's so easy. Just ignore him."

"I have a question," announces Mr. O'Meara.

Jeanne glances into the mirror. "Don't answer him, Sarah."

"*What. Is. It?*" Sarah's teeth are clenched. "You better NOT be joking. I'm warning you!"

"Why didn't the two fours want any dinner?"

"Jim," Jeanne pleads. "C'mon."

"I'm angry! My blood is BOILING!"

"Don't shout, Sarah," Jeanne says.

"Because they already eight," Mr. O'Meara says.

And so it goes. Past Fort Wingate. Over the Continental Divide. Past El Malpais, the badlands.

Albert is in my charge for the weekend. He steers clear of the conversation; he does not, in fact, seem to register a word of it. He sits between Mr. O'Meara and me, in the back seat, and watches Metallica videos on my phone with the volume turned low. Albert is twelve, sixty-five pounds, and about four feet and five inches, with black hair past his shoulders. A strand of his hair is tipped with cake frosting, which is a mystery, because I haven't seen cake all day.

Albert is a student of mine. He had some rough times earlier in the year. A classmate bullied Albert on the sly, always when I wasn't looking. Albert never said a word. Then, one day in October, he stood from his desk, strode across the front of the class, hoisted a twenty-gallon metal trash can and, without missing a step on his way out, lofted it backward over his shoulder. There was little I could do but watch the can sail through the air and crash onto an unoffending student's desk, injuring the boy's wrist, though slightly.

Albert disappeared after that, for several weeks. When he returned, he was thinner, with a greenish pallor and black rings beneath his eyes. And very quiet. At the start of each class, he would push his worksheets off his desk, throw himself into a slouch, and cross his arms. So I'd give him loose-leaf paper to sketch on. Horses and clowns, mainly, some drawn with admirable precision, others more tangled.

"Teacher," Albert asks as we pass through Laguna Pueblo. "Do Korean people eat dogs?"

I don't know what set him on this line of inquiry, but he's troubled by it. Judging by the worry in his eyes, much depends on this issue.

I try to give him a handle. "In places where people are poor, they probably eat what they can." In truth, I don't know a thing about it, but I keep talking. "Albert," I say, "it's not a big deal." Dogs have been on human beings' menu for a long time. In some countries, I tell him, people eat camels. "People eat marmot, sheep cud. Snake meat. Spiders."

I recalled a summer night during Peace Corps service in Mongolia. Several men, stripped to their shorts and sweating, were seated in a circle around a wok brimming with horse guts. "You know, Albert," I say, "boiled horse blood has the texture of tofu."

None of this matters. He turns back to the phone. "How do you spell Korea?" he asks.

I ask him to find some music videos instead. Later, alerted by his secretive manner, I catch a glimpse of the video he is watching, amateur footage of a hopeless dog chained to a cinder block in a trashed lot. When I take the phone away, Albert hugs his chest and glowers at his knees.

At the University of New Mexico sports stadium, coaches in neon-green shirts push wheelchairs around the track as the chairs' occupants wave to the cheering crowd. During the next event, the announcer encourages the participants on the four-hundred-meter walk. *Let's show some love to the walker in blue*, the voice says as the man makes the final turn into the stretch.

Way to go!

It's hot at 10:00 a.m., and the man nears the finish line in a panting sweat.

Good Lord, don't have a heart attack! the announcer says, drawing laughter from the stands. The man is greeted with hugs at the finish. *Just kidding!*

The athlete seated beside me is a local kid. He likes high school, he says, but winces when the talk turns on the other boys' dirty mouths. "They say the F-word," he tells me. "The D-word. The N-word."

The four-hundred-meter walk isn't over yet. Sarah makes the final turn five minutes behind the winner. Her half-hearted efforts are met with cheers and applause, which she accepts with cool disdain. She ambles across the finish line, unflappable in yellow socks and a green shade visor, the sort worn by mob accountants and casino dealers. She has not deigned to break a sweat.

The kid beside me chats away. His mind's on school. "The C-word. The S-word. The B-word. . . ."

Beyond the stadium, beyond the university buildings and trees, a single mountain of bare rock is visible, amber-colored in the sere light of a May noon. The desert's sudden proximity startles me. Here, in the middle of the city, surrounded by trees and office buildings and overpasses, it is easy to forget where we are. I look about at my fellow spectators, at the picnic baskets and umbrellas, the grass-covered soccer field. No one else, it seems, has noticed the intrusion.

In stealth, the earth's deserts are spreading, encroaching on us while we tend to other matters. Now, the desert has insinuated itself within Albuquerque city limits, only a short walk away: a sand patrol probing the city's defenses, a reconnaissance-in-dust. Desert silence is a stalking silence, and each year finds the sand, as the poet wrote, "one long, slow step nearer."[1]

These apocalyptic fancies come and go. That night at the hotel, Albert falls asleep in a mess of Skittle wrappers and muffin crumbs, and all's well with the world once more.

III. The Manifest of Don Luís de Velasco

"Manifest made by Captain Don Luís de Velasco of the goods, arms, and horses which he is taking to serve his Majesty," as declared before, and drawn up by, the royal clerk and secretary of the expedition, Juan Pérez de Donis, at the "mines of Casco where is encamped the army of his Majesty which is going to the conquest and pacification of the provinces of New Mexico, on the nineteenth day of May, 1597":[2]

> First . . . a standard in figured white Castilian silk, with fringes and trimmings of gold and crimson silk.
>
> Item: A silver lance, in its handle, for the exercise of his office as captain, with tassels of old and yellow and purple silk.
>
> Item: For the said purpose three complete suits of armor, to arm himself and two other soldiers in coat of mail . . .
>
> Item: Three calivers, with their large and small powder horns, firelocks, bullet screws, moulds . . .
>
> Item: Three sets of horse armor of buckskin, lined with undressed leather, for the flanks, foreheads, breasts, necks—all, without anything lacking.
>
> Item: A halberd, garnished with yellow velvet and purple tassels, and all studded with nails . . .
>
> Item: Thirty war horses of different brands and marks . . .

Item: A sword and a gilded dagger with their waist belts stitched with purple, yellow, and white silk.

Item: One broadsword with shoulder belt, and two shields for defense against arrows.

Item: Two trooper saddles of Córdovan leather . . .

Item: One bed with two mattresses, a coverlet, sheets, pillow-cases, pillows . . .

Item: He is taking in his service two Spanish servants, from eighteen to twenty years old.

Item: One suit of blue Italian velvet trimmed with wide gold passementerie, consisting of doublet, breeches, and green silk stockings with blue garters with points of gold lace . . .

Item: Another suit of rose-colored lustrous Castilian satin . . . and garters of striped rose-colored taffeta.

Item: Another suit of straw-colored Castilian satin . . .

Item: Another suit of purple Castilian cloth . . .

Item: Another suit of chestnut-colored London cloth . . .

Item: Another suit of Chinese flowered silk . . .

Item: Two doublets of kid dressed in Castile, one from the royal city . . .

Item: Another doublet of royal lion skin . . .

Item: Six handkerchiefs of Rouen linen . . .

Item: Eight pairs of Córdovan leather boots, six white pairs, and four black, and four pairs of laced gaiters.

Item: Two hats, one black, trimmed around the crown with a silver cord, with black, purple, and white feathers, and the other gray, with yellow and purple feathers.

Item: Another hat of purple taffeta . . .

Item: . . . some Moorish spurs with tassels and cords of silk.

Item: Fifty yards of striped canvas of Michoacan bindweed for a tent . . .

IV. The "Mission Province"

The early Spanish entradas into this land in the sixteenth century never yielded enough plunder to cover expenses. The bootless hardships of these northern ventures, when contrasted with the wild successes at Mexico and Peru, mocked the soldiers' fantasies. As the decades passed, and the poverty of the land (as the invaders reckoned poverty) became apparent, and the cities of gold receded deeper into the conquerors' dreams, New Mexico became a "mission province," a colony supported primarily for the greater glory of God, and not, like the silver cities of Nueva Vizcaya, for the enrichment of the crown. And because the priests believed that Christ would return only when all the peoples of the earth had been converted to the cross, they hastened to complete the work.

A century after Coronado's expeditions, New Mexico was, in the eyes of Spain, a backwater. Santa Fe lay fifteen hundred miles to the north of Mexico City, at the end of a trail that led through the Jornada del Muerto, the "dead man's journey," the stone wilderness west of the White Sands. The beleaguered inmates of northern outposts and missions might wait three years, and sometimes more, between arrivals of the little convoys from Mexico bearing food and weapons, liturgical paraphernalia, and the inevitable news of wars in Europe. Volunteers for frontier duty were scarce, and for this reason replacements for the garrisons were often fugitives or criminals who sometimes arrived at their posts in chains. The vicious character of settlers and soldiers was a constant theme of the priests' reports.

New colonists were lured by promises of wealth that rarely materialized, and the colony was kept barely alive, for decades, on a thin gruel of poor intelligence, half-truths, and mirages of pearl fisheries and magic kingdoms. In 1602, the Viceroy Gaspar de Zuñiga y Acevedo, Conde de Monterrey, wrote to King Felipe III that in New Mexico "poverty is everywhere," and that it was difficult to persuade anyone to go to the province, "for neither will the food be lavish nor the clothing dignified."[3]

In the remotest missions, where six or seven years might pass without a word or a face from New Spain, the friars huddled by their piñon fires. "Suffice it to say," wrote one Father Benavides, nearly a century after Coronado had come and gone, "that when we are saying Mass, we keep a brazier burning on each side of the chalice; even with this precaution . . . the wine still freezes. Every winter a great number of Indians out in the country are found frozen, and many Spaniards have their ears, feet and hands frozen."[4] They nevertheless managed to establish mission schools, where Spanish and Indian boys were catechized along with, increasingly, mestizo children. Gradually, the time came when visitors could no longer discern the bloodlines in the pupils' faces.

The Spaniards' identities—along with their peacock plumes and blue stockings, their Italian velvets and silken banners—faded with intermarriage and time, as the high desert wind and sun wore away, by imperceptible degrees, the defining edges of the invaders and their habits.

V. Nicolás de Aguilar: An Inventory

One Nicolás de Aguilar, thirty-six years old, an officer and a district mayor in the Santa Fe region, was transported to Mexico City to face charges of murder and heresy. The following report is the First Hearing of the Inquisition, which took place on April 12, 1663:[5]

He is a man of large body, coarse, and somewhat brown; he says he is thirty-six years old. He wears a gabardine of buff and black wool, a doublet of white cloth embroidered with blue wool, trousers of dark red flannel with small points of black wool lace, blue woolen stockings, a cotton neckcloth adorned with drawn work, and shoes of buckskin from New Mexico. Apparently he brought nothing else with him. In a white wooden box, the key of which he handed over there was also found:

Item 5. An old cotton shirt, adorned with drawn work.

Item 6. Another cloth shirt, worn out.

Item 7. A shirt of ordinary Rouen linen.

Item 12. One pair of shoes of Córdovan leather, worn out.

Item 13. A book, entitled, "Catechism in the Castilian and Timuquana languages." Inside of this was another very small book, entitled, "Instructions for examining the conscience."

Item 14. A bar of soap and a little *alucema* [a medicinal plant supposed to lower fevers] wrapped in an old black rag.

Item 15. An antelope skin muffler lined with yellow linen.

Item 16. A cloth containing, apparently, roots of dry grass, which he said they call bear grass in New Mexico, used for curing fevers.

Item 17. Three small pieces of dried grass roots, which he said is called *manso* grass, and is good for healing wounds.

Item 18. A fair-sized bag of relics . . .

Item 19. A little printed copy of the four Gospels.

Item 21. A rosary strung on *coyole* wire [strand of fruit fiber?], having large beads, and a little silver cross.

Item 22. A very small and old book bound with small black boards, which had no title at the beginning, and seemed to consist, in the middle, of exercises and reflections.

Item 24. A very old black hat.

Item 25. A buckskin bag within which is a cotton pillow filled with sheep's wool.

Item 26. A mattress of coarse black and white stuff, filled with sheep's wool.

This Aguilar, who arrived in manacles in Mexico City, stood at several removes—in dress, in speech, in worldly knowledge—from the wealthy young adventurer, Don Luís de Velasco, mentioned above, who headed north from the Casco mines in May 1597. As historian Andrew Knaut, observes, "an immense cultural and genetic gap had emerged to separate Velasco from his counterpart."[6] Like the prodigal of the old story, Velasco, the rich man's son decked in ostrich plumes and Chinese silks, departed his father's house in search of riches and adventure. Nearly seventy years passed before his revenant returned, in the person of Nicolás de Aguilar. But, unlike the prodigal of the story, no one was waiting to place a ring on his finger, and no fatted calf was fetched to welcome him.

At the time of his arrest, Aguilar was representative of a sizable portion of the colonial population. To men and women like him had passed the keys to the Kingdom of Cibola.

The old dreams died hard. Friars and soldiers set out from the settlements on expeditions that led them ever deeper into the continental interior, in search of the evanescent cities of gold. The half-starved survivors of these journeys recorded vast herds of animals they called cattle, the "vacas de Cibola": the American bison. They told of plains covered with the red-and-white tepees of nomads. The sight of Apaches on the move—in convoys of hundreds of pack dogs, each dragging a loaded travois—provided an unforgettable spectacle to the Spaniards.

But the soldiers returned to their missions and high-desert towns and ranches. And those rich plains, of which they had caught only glimpses, were destined to fall into the hands of a more numerous breed of invaders from the east.

VI. Origins

The Navajo people had inhabited many worlds before emerging into this one, Mr. Begaye told me. We sat in his classroom—the last people in the school building, at 4:00 p.m. on the Friday before Christmas break—and talked about time. Mr. Begaye said it was tough to talk about certain things in English. There's so much Latin in it, he said, and Latin's a very rational language. Comes to that, he added, it's not a whole lot easier to talk about in Navajo. There just aren't enough words for things, no matter who's talking.

On the classroom walls were diagrams of the Navajo zodiac, cosmological symbols of animals, lightning, patterns conjuring eternity. Dim approximations of these designs might be found carved into the center post of a ger in the Gobi, or on a temple bell in western China, the regions from which an ancient people began a long walk that brought them, over the course of millennia, to this place. (A long walk, though not to be confused with the "Long Walk" of more recent memory, in 1864, when thousands of Navajos were forcibly removed from their lands in the present-day Four Corners region to Fort Sumner in eastern New Mexico. Hundreds perished during that two-month winter march.)

If it did occur, little trace of the ancient passage remains. Although the Bering Land Bridge theory was presented as settled science in my grade-school science text, the evidence has always been scant and inconclusive.

This dissension among scientists doesn't trouble Mr. Begaye. I cannot determine his thoughts on this matter. Perhaps the whole issue of time is beside the point. To underscore my confusion, he lets me in on some troubling news. Weapons dating to the thirteenth century, including shields and cotton armor bearing the Christian cross, were discovered in a remote canyon of the Colorado River. The feds got wind of it, he tells me, confiscated the gear, and closed the canyon off to visitors. A column of Crusaders, perhaps, who went catastrophically astray on the road to Jericho—who knows?

Time and space, unfixed and concurrent, replete with possibility.

To what extent is this place, the present-day Navajo Nation, considered a home, and to what extent is it just a way station, one of many, between here and here? Mr. Begaye's answers are vague, because my questions are ill-considered, perhaps impertinent, certainly not to the point. I wish to ask thoughtful questions, for there is much I want to know. But I don't know how to begin.

> There were no sun, no moon, no stars, but there were four great snow-covered peaks on the horizon in each of the cardinal directions.
> ("Creation of First Man and First Woman")[7]

Having been driven, according to one story, from three successive worlds because of their quarreling and unfaithful ways, the people emerged into the Fourth World, the Middle Place—a region bounded by four sacred mountains—the Place from Which All Life Emerges. It was here they encountered others not unlike themselves, the Pueblo, and here they found a home.

I set this story (one of many variations on the theme) beside the scientific version of events. Years of Western education have impressed on me certain habits of perception that, at fifty, I am only beginning to unlearn. By the light of that education, the range of possible truth extends, essentially, only so far as I can see or hear; this, despite a hundred daily reminders of these senses' fallibility. That my eyes can "deceive" me is a revealing idiom, for the eyes are capable not only of error but of downright mischief. And yet I persist in my reliance on them, for I've been taught to mistrust my imagination. These habits of thought, materialist and reasonable, inculcated across fifteen generations of my ancestors, have wrought immense evil in the world, and my continued dependence on them is the result of indolence and a fearful obedience to wisdoms received uncritically and *on faith*—which is ironic, given so much enlightened disdain for religion. Modern Western philosophy and education represent tragic failures of nerve, and my wholesale, incurious subscription to them is a failure of will.

I've proven myself a slavish thinker; I see that now. And so, putting aside those timeworn modes of understanding—which I can do in rare lucid moments—I see that one event can bear multiple truths. In this way are many difficulties resolved, and I thank God that the horizons of ignorance (if only by a degree or two, if only at this later stage) begin to recede.

The Land Bridge theory is attractive, I have to believe, in part because it is a tale of a journey of majestic dimensions, and a story without a journey is seldom worth hearing. Here are questions. What drove people from the plains of north-central Asia to this continent? Was it a forced migration, a search for refuge from tribes of freebooters and raiders? A search for better pasturage merely? Or a working-out of some communal salvation, the resolution of an inscrutable destiny handed down in songs, or written in the stars?

In that place from which they purportedly came, mountains, snow-covered nine months a year, ring the horizon. The cobalt sky admits of ice-bearing clouds that seldom rain, but diffract the sunlight into violets, emeralds, and rosy golds. To spend time in that land is to be touched by the sere light as with an exotic strain of delirium.

I recall an old woman at dawn, in the western Gobi, with a bowl and a spoon, casting milk and a blessing to each of the four directions (which are marked, in another world far to the east, by four mountains decked in snow and legend).

The story goes something like this. From the ancestral lands in present Siberia, Mongolia, and Kazakhstan, a people (or peoples) traversed a tundra of darkness and ice, of midnight suns and howling seas, on a migration that lasted generations. There is no chapter in human history that taxes my imagination so much as the story of the great Beringian walk. I can envision Polynesian sea voyages; I can comprehend Hunnish tribes crashing like waves across Europe; I can follow the conjectured routes of Rift Valley hunters as they fan out across Arabia and central Africa. The land bridge crossing, however, occurred in a region of tectonic activity where the diurnal cycle of day and night, familiar to most life on earth, does not obtain. At the time of the migration, strange creatures lived there, such as American lions, giant sloths, camelids, and mastodons. I envision a journey across a treeless land undulant as the sea, a land studded with immense boulders livid with orange and yellow lichen, a rolling land green as Scotland during the brief summers. There, distant ranges of ice-bound peaks serrate the skyline.

"I would like to have heard the voices of those ancients who crossed the Bering Bridge to the North American continent thirty thousand years ago," N. Scott Momaday writes in *Man Made of Words* (1997). "Certainly there were storytellers among them, singers, makers of prayers, what we call poets." He recounts the words of the Sioux Buffalo Dance, which seems to commemorate the hardships of an old passage, and which preserves an eerie memory of ice:[8]

In the north
the wind
blows
they are walking
the hail
beats
they are walking

These thoughts draw me back to Genesis. Perhaps the maker or makers of the Eden myth were inspired by yet older stories of an agonizing passage from some ancestral homeland to the present one, a journey that became allegorized, over time and in countless iterations, in a tale of two "orchard thieves" (Melville's term) named Adam and Eve, who were banished from a life of ease and plenty to a world of numbers, work, and death. In the manner of much storytelling, the real journey was transformed into a spiritual one. In the most recent version, the ignition of consciousness—occurring in tandem with submission to a tyrannical and empirical ego—attended the thieves' banishment and constituted a goodly portion of their punishment.

For the exiles of the Genesis story, the world they were compelled to enter, as the price of obstinacy, was a world without negation or affirmation, a world indifferent and multitudinous. Across this world streamed perplexity and pain endlessly. In time, their descendants crafted a religion from scraps of storm-lit visions, and the fractured memories of lost homes.

What, by comparison, set the Beringian migrants wandering? Their arrival here in this high desert of sere violet skies must have seemed, after that subarctic journey, like trading one planet for another. Perhaps this informs the creation stories of the Diné, in which the people arrive at a succession of worlds before emerging at last into this one.

These memories, surviving as stories, have outlasted stone. They are the oldest living things on earth.

My mind counts backward and understands the passage of time as a more or less unbroken succession of moments receding in perspective haze. For the Diné, perhaps, there is not a counting backward, and no haze, but an eternal arrival at the beginning.

The terrible irony, as the scholar Joni Adamson points out, is that this place of arrival, the Place from Which All Life Emerges, is now the site of enormous coal-fired power plants, mountains and mesas blasted and gouged for uranium, and some of the world's largest open-pit mines, all of which have poisoned the water, the land, and the air, sickening and killing people, animals, and plants.[9]

This is what I want to ask Mr. Begaye: Did the people conceive of those previous homelands as existing in time? Or as places they might, by taking thought, revisit any time they wished, if only in dreams? Is this high place of transient waters, of wind and stone and snow, the same place they left so many years ago, a place not to be found on any map?

Is home, I want to know, a place in time? In our hearts only? Has it been prepared for us, or must we build it? In this life, or the next?

Have we been here since the beginning? Have I been here all the while?

But it's time to pack up and go. Mr. Begaye has to get to his second job at the tire shop. Teachers, he says, don't make a lot of money, you know. Merry Christmas!

VII. White Sands Desert

Looking east from Augustin Pass, high in the Organ Mountains, you can see the Sacramento Mountains, eighty miles distant, suspended above the horizon. Between the Organs and the Sacramentos stretches the vast Tularosa Basin, and there you find the White Sands Missile Range. At a roadside historical marker, the traveler can stop to read an account of the history of atomic weaponry. Behind the information boards is an impotent, forty-foot-tall Nike missile, relic of the arms-race era, slightly canted on its stand like an Advent candle left on the mantle till spring.

I duck my head and let go on a long glide down to the desert floor: no brakes, no pedals for twenty miles. In late afternoon, I reach the White Sands Monument entrance, where I pay five dollars to pitch my bivouac tent in the backcountry.

That night, the moon rises in a floury haze and casts a blue light on the gypsum dunes. Stars glow in their shallow beds. Seated on a tall dune, I bury my hands in sand that leaves a viscous, gritty film on the fingers.

An hour after sundown, the fighter-bombers emerge from the air base near Alamogordo. A flight of three rises in a flat arc, afterburners blazing. One after the other, they veer skyward, then bank south. I crack the seal on a booter of vodka and lean back.

All around, the white dunes crest and plunge in stillness.

VIII. Flora and Fauna

In the high forests of Ponderosa pine, in autumn, the afternoon is well advanced by the time the sap begins to run. When it does, the forest fills with an odor at once sweet and stringent, tinted with cinnamon and witch hazel, more of a taste than a smell.

The pine bark is warm as horsehide, dry as dust to the touch. Within an hour, as the air cools, the sap will cease to run. Then, the shadows will daub and blot the scent, leaving the chitter of late-foraging birds as recompense.

As winds mill in distant corners of the afternoon, the forest becomes an Irish wake, a timbered parlor of mournful little quarrels. Then the winds cease, and the silence rings in my ears with a zinc-inflected hiss, like a mild burn that simmers as it cools, or the sound of two wet stones rubbed very slowly together.

I find a bed of needles to lie on, stretch out on my back, ankles together, and bury my hands in my pockets. Above the pines' crowns, the long, attenuated clouds are planed and blunted, bright as pine board, heartwood-yellow-colored, fixed deep in the sky like the broken rafters of a deserted palace.

I think about God sometimes. How did the Mind that conceived the black-eared Abert's squirrel and the Steller's jay and the claret cup cactus, ever come to be identified with an elderly narcolept who just wants us to, of all things, *behave*?

In spring and autumn, the wind crashes through the woods, and the boughs pitch and creak and snap. The branches wave, which allows sunlight to pass down, branch to branch. In this manner, every needle on every twig on every branch is afforded, so to speak, its moment in the sun. This is how the whole is nourished—every leaf, every cell—by the wind.

In an old Navajo story, it is the wind that gives life to First Woman and First Man, "and it is the wind that comes out of our mouths now that gives us life."[10] This story echoes the Mosaic creation story, when “darkness was upon the face of the deep, And the Spirit of God moved upon the face of the waters”: *tenebrae erant super faciem abyssi: et spiritus Dei ferebatur super aquas.*[11]

God, says the Psalmist, “bringeth the wind out of his treasuries,” which is a pretty picture.[12] I imagine a lonely widower opening a carven sea chest at dawn, selecting the choicest lightning flashes and the rarest breezes to adorn the day withal.

“The wynde bloweth where he listeth,” says the author of John’s Gospel in Tyndale’s 1526 translation, “and thou hearest his sounde but canst nott tell whence he cometh and whether he goeth. So is every man that is boren of the sprete.”[13]

Spiritus, wind, breath.

“When this ceases to blow,” reads the Navajo story, “we die.”

IX. Society & People (II)

On the morning of the big race, Albert prepares by watching cartoons in the hotel room. He takes his meds with an entire pack of Starburst. We finish two complimentary coffees and I fetch us two more from the lobby.

Albert earns two medals at the Games, and he sends pictures of himself wearing his awards to his guardian at the group home, where he lives with his sister, Albertina. In the evening we join a couple hundred participants and volunteers at Cliffs Amusement Park, where Albert discovers that Special Olympics athletes are, for one day only, allowed to cut to the front of every line. This leads to six turns at the Demolition Disco, his bumper-car rides fueled by ICEEs and Flamin’ Hot Cheetos. There’s a barbecue dinner, a dance with a DJ, and a journey on the old-time train.

Maria, an athlete, is crying. She is petrified of the train, believing that it will climb high and go fast like the roller coasters do. The attendants watch in dismay as Ms. L and Ms. F and I carry and coax and pull her aboard the toy passenger carriage, where Sarah is waiting.

“C’mon, Maria,” Sarah says gently, wearily. “It’s just a darned old train.”

At last we're underway, rolling through the gathering twilight, winding beneath the soaring coasters, along the chain link fence of the park limits, past knots of park-goers waving ironically at crossings. The train enters the old mine shaft, where effigies of Forty-Niners, poorly stitched and bleeding straw, pan gold or languish in jail cells littered with popcorn cartons and Mountain Dew bottles.

"It's just a darned old train," Sarah says, over and over, in a tranquil monotone to calm her friend. It's just a darned old train, Maria.

It's just a darned old train.

Albert wakes up on the last day in a sour mood, and he will not get out of bed. I pull the covers from his grip and he curses me, after his manner. A hot coffee with extra sugar and a donut fail to entice him, and I have to call for assistance.

Ms. D has more patience than I do. I must not forget to give thanks for her, and for the others, and to pray for some portion of the loving-kindness and cheerful generosity they possess in abundance. Their gentle natures make all they do seem easy, but I know it is not so. Theirs is a patience borne of years of shared sorrows and small—often very small—victories.

After the closing ceremonies, as we ride back to the hotel, Ms. D rubs her knees. "When I was young, I used to laugh at those old ladies who always complained about how much their feet hurt," she says with a smile. "Not no more!" Ms. D has volunteered at the Games for thirty years, and she shepherds the athletes through their days with imperturbable grace, cool efficiency, a joke for every difficulty, and a comforting word for every worry. Now past retirement, she has taken on a new mission: organizing a statewide effort to protect LGBTQ youth from bullying at New Mexico schools. The current state laws are inadequate to the point of cruelty, she tells me. She aims to change that. "God guided me to this opportunity, and I think I can do some good. I'm not ready to pack it in yet."

On the trip back, while the kids sleep, I read a book by a man named

Berdyaev. He wrote *The Destiny of Man* in Germany and France in the mid-1930s, in exile from Stalin's terror. Berdyaev writes of love—not the flimsy, egocentric sort that bubbles up from the "bad infinity" of the selfish will, but a different kind of love.

> The greatest mystery of life is that satisfaction is felt not by those who take and make demands but by those who give and make sacrifices. In them alone the energy of life does not fail, and this is precisely what is meant by creativeness. Therefore, the positive mystery of life is to be found in love, in sacrificial, giving, creative love.[14]

I am reading Berdyaev's book for the second time, and it pains me that such simple truths should demand revisiting at all. So I ask myself whether it is to ignorance (which I may amend) or to a spiritual deficit (which I may not amend) that I should attribute my difficulties.

Love is paradoxical, say the old books, over and over in their ways. If you want to gain, lose; if you want to obtain happiness, do not seek it, never think of it, and forget the very word; if you want to acquire strength, manifest it. Give it away, and it will be returned manifold.

On the ride back to Gallup, Sarah sleeps. Mr. O'Meara sleeps. Ms. B and Ms. L chat quietly in the front seat. Among the passengers in the back, only Albert is awake, watching videos on my phone. He has found footage of plane crashes.

To me, there is something almost comical about a plane crash. Perhaps it is the image of a thing so categorically out of its element, like a ghost in the broad light of day, or the devil above ground whistling for his lost cow.

No longer high above, where it should be—cruising in abstract silence at thirty thousand feet, as is proper—but suddenly here among us, aimed at an eighty-degree angle to a soybean field. In a jetliner's improbable proximity, earthbound objects such as trees and barns become smaller by magnitudes, suddenly changeable and unreal, like the beguiling little depot buildings, so lovingly crafted, in a model-train display.

Albert watches one bit of footage over and over, a loop that concludes a fraction of a second prior to impact. He replays, again and again, the final five hundred feet of the plane's flight, the final second of the many unseen lives on board. Over and over, the moment unravels; over and over, the plane pauses just above the earth. And though we both know how it ends, we keep watching, wondering, perhaps, if this time things might turn out different.

The Rock Cycle

Shortly after the turn of the sixteenth century, in the years when Michelangelo was overseeing the stonecutters at the Carrera marble quarry, Leonardo da Vinci was gathering fossils in the hills around Florence. He was among the first Europeans to realize that fossils were not flotsam of the Deluge or cosmic pranks, but the results of geologic processes. The discovery had been intended for a proposed *Treatise on Water* but, like most of his scientific thought, the work remained unfinished. Here is what he wrote at the time:

> Since things are much more ancient than letters, it is no marvel if, in our day, no records exist of these seas having covered so many countries; and if moreover such record ever existed, the wars, the conflagrations, the deluges of the waters, the changes of languages and of laws, have consumed every vestige of the past. But sufficient for us is the testimony of things produced in the salt waters and found again in high mountains, far from the seas of today.[1]

From the presence of fossils at high altitudes, da Vinci concluded that the land was at one time covered by water.

> And the peaks of the Apennines stood up in this sea like islands surrounded by salt water . . . and above the plains of Italy where flocks of birds are flying today, fishes were wont to wander in large shoals.[2]

His observations are presented with such casual assurance, it is easy to miss the profound visionary leap involved.

we find no vestige of a beginning, no prospect of an end[3]

Nearly three centuries would pass before this insight would be codified by the Scottish geologist and farmer James Hutton. In an abstract of a dissertation titled *Concerning the System of the Earth, its Duration and Stability*, submitted to the Royal Society on July 4, 1785, Hutton proposed the theory that the present aspect of the land is the result of transformations occurring over vast tracts of time.

The new theory, published in 1788 in the two-volume *Theory of the Earth* (and corroborated by his successor Charles Lyell in *Principles of Geology*, 1830), reflected Hutton's belief that "the past history of our globe must be explained by what can be seen to be happening now."[4] The once-for-all cataclysm of the Noachian Flood—whose receding waters putatively left, like a global tidewrack, boulders visibly strewn across the plains of the northern hemisphere—was replaced by a gradual process of renewal and decay.

For twenty-five years, Hutton made detailed observations of rock layers revealed in canal beds, mountains, and coastlines in Scotland, England, and Scandinavia. The fixed and static earth of Genesis eroded under his observations, and a dynamic one emerged in its place. "As *it is not in human record*," he wrote,

> *but in natural history*, that we are to look for the means of ascertaining what has already been, it is here proposed to examine the appearances of the earth, in order to be informed of operations which have been transacted in time past. It is thus that, from principles of natural philosophy, *we may arrive at some knowledge* of order and system in the economy of this globe, and may *form a rational opinion* with regard to the course of nature, or to events which are in time to happen.[5]

Hutton's work demolished the Mosaic chronology. Paradoxically, by assigning an incalculable antiquity to the earth, he brought the earth to life. As the American anthropologist Loren Eiseley observed, Hutton "had come upon the secret of the relatively perpetual youth of the planet."[6] The cursed and stricken earth of Genesis was quickened. (Notably, as a young university student, Hutton wrote his doctoral thesis on the circulation of the blood.)

In founding the modern concept of geologic time—or "deep time," as it came to be known—Hutton wrote that the "solid parts of the present land appear in general, to have been composed of the productions of the sea . . ."

> Hence we find reason to conclude:
>
> 1st, That the land on which we rest is not simple and original, but that it is a composition, and had been formed by the operation of second causes.
>
> 2nd, That before the present land was made, there had subsisted a world composed of sea and land, in which were tides and currents, with such operations at the bottom of the sea as now take place. And,
>
> Lastly, That while the present land was forming at the bottom of the ocean, the former land maintained plants and animals; at least the sea was then inhabited by animals, in a similar manner as it is at present.[7]

Here, translated into eighteenth-century Academese (though retaining a visual chime) is da Vinci's observation. The insight defied Scripture—and common sense. The suggestion that the hills and valleys had not been there for all time—that they were involved in unending cycles of sedimentation and uplift—was absurd to most of Hutton's contemporaries, and would be absurd to us were we not compelled to attend earth-science classes in the ninth grade. As Eiseley notes, "Hutton's axiom that the understanding of present forces is the key to the past is now the basis of the natural sciences."[8] For natural sciences, and for history.

All this took generations to seep into popular consciousness, and Hutton's work went widely unnoticed beyond the circle of scholars at the Royal Society. As surely as the work of Kepler and Newton and Galileo had broken the bounds of space, Hutton's observations broke the bounds of time. This expansion of the age of the earth provided needed scope for impending evolutionary theories as well, which required an immense temporal stage to achieve plausibility.

For centuries, the presence of seashells on mountaintops posed a logical difficulty. Human intuition, commonly tuned to anomalies, had often suspected that fossils were keys to old secrets. The Greeks, bound to no biblical chronologies, could ruminate freely. Ovid, in his *Metamorphoses*, observes the presence of seashells on sandy plains "with never an ocean or a ship in sight."[9] Eratosthenes, as recorded in Strabo's *Geography*, was intrigued by "the abundance of cockle, oyster, and scallop shells" found at higher altitudes, and he observed that "salt-water lakes are frequently seen far inland."[10] But neither was able, as far as I can tell, to draw any conclusions from this. (Eratosthenes's talents lay in another direction. With the aid of an assistant, a short stick, a deep well, and the noon sun, he estimated, to within a few hundred miles, the circumference of the earth. But that's a different story.)

In the West, such audacious speculation ended with Constantine. The Latin Fathers, as Marjorie Hope Nicolson observes, were "more concerned with Genesis than geology."[11] Augustine suspected that fossil teeth belonged to the "giants" that are mentioned in Genesis 6: "There were giants in the earth in those days," when "the sons of God saw the daughters of men, and that they were fair."

Andrew White, in *A History of the Warfare of Science with Theology* (1896), records that fossils were believed to be "sports of Nature" by late medieval and early modern thinkers. Fossils were "models of His works approved or rejected by the great Artificer"; "outlines of future creations"; or "objects placed in the strata to bring to naught human curiosity." Others held the opinion that fossils were the products of "fatty matter set into a fermentation by heat" or of a "lapidific juice"; of a "seminal air" or a "tumultuous movement of terrestrial exhalations."[12]

The ancient speculative spirit found new life, though tempered, with the advent of the New Learning in the seventeenth century. No legitimate natural philosopher could evade the problems posed by the discovery of marine fossils at high altitudes, just as, in preceding centuries, no legitimate theologian could evade the question of why God made the world *in time*.

Men suspected astral influences, attributing the existence of fossils to malign conjunctions of stars. Tales were spun from whole cloth: some blamed the demons who lurked in mines;[13] some claimed fossils were counterfeits fashioned by the devil; and others believed they were created by God to try men's faith. An older term for fossils, "formed stones," betrays a suspicion of supernatural premeditation (malevolent or otherwise).

As late as the latter half of the seventeenth century, Robert Burton, the librarian of Christ's Church College at Cambridge, wondered what some voyager into the "bowels of the earth" might discover:

> do stones and metals grow there still? how come fir-trees to be digged out from the tops of hills, as in our mosses and marshes all over Europe? How come they to dig up fish-bones, shells, beams, iron-works, many fathoms underground, and anchors in mountains far remote from all seas?[14]

It would be a mistake to overstate this curiosity for fossils. For most of humanity, through most of history, necessarily viewing the earth from their workaday perspective, the facts of geologic change do not often intrude on the demands of survival. As Hutton noted, "the shepherd thinks the mountain, on which he feeds his flock, to have always been there."[15] And for sound practical reasons, so do most of us.

> While these bits of rock were buried in the earth, civilizations rose and fell, mountain ranges bloomed and disappeared like smoke. But to the rocks nothing mattered but the steady transformation of parent element to daughter, a steady nuclear ticking that continued unvarying and unperturbed. (*Ages in Chaos*, Stephen Baxter)[16]

Here, in the Indus River valley, as I'd learned in grade school, was where human beings first settled in towns and raised crops. I recalled the valley's happy alias, the "cradle of civilization," from seventh grade social studies, and I searched from the bus window for signs of its textbook significance. As a twelve-year-old, I imagined a broad and placid stream flowing past prosperous, palisaded towns. I imagined figures dressed in white gowns, engaged in homely arts like spinning and weaving. This, as everyone knows, is how history began.

But the river didn't agree with the textbook. It seemed younger than it ought, a yellow torrent pitching between sheer rock banks, muscular as a young bull, leaping from its bed where the channel doglegged. Mountaintops rose from their shadow-filled valleys like atolls from a violet sea. As the bus reeled and bottomed, and the passengers swayed in unison like blades of river grass, I opened a geology text I'd found in a book stall in Srinagar, Kashmir.

> As soon as these heights were attained by the rocks, nature's opposing forces of denudation and erosion started working on them, these subaerial agencies never allowing any heights for long on the earth's surface![17]

The Eurasian plate had risen as the Indian subcontinent slipped beneath it, creating the Himalaya. The road we traveled on traversed the seam, so to speak, between India and Central Asia.

The region of Zanskar straddles that seam. The name fits the nature of the place: desiccated, treeless, riven by rare storms and violent fluctuations in temperature and the ordinary epochal upheavals. On a theoretical level, I know that the processes of orogeny occur within measurable temporal parameters, but my mind becomes less efficient as I extend its scope. I can readily imagine local events unfolding within slender bands of time, incremental lapses such as the passage of winter to spring, or the diurnal swing between heat and frost. Sunshine and ice, drought and snow, the long seasons in which no precipitation occurs to check the slow return to dust: these shifts can be comprehended. Beyond that lie propositions that I take largely on faith. "Zanskar lies within the Danger Zone of the earth," the author writes. I can believe that.

> And God said vnto Nóah, An end of all flesh is come before me: for the earth is filled with crueltie through them: and beholde, I will destroye them with the earth. (Genesis, vi.13)[18]

To understand the land in terms of human pain and violence is an old habit. Because you ate of the tree, God tells Adam, "Curséd is the ground for thy sake." Other translations prefer "earth" to "ground." For generations of Christian theologians, much depended on whether the whole world, or only its soil, was cursed. Milton, in Book IX of *Paradise Lost*, took the more drastic view:

> Earth felt the wound, and Nature from her seat,
> Sighing through all her works, gave sign of woe
> That all was lost.[19]

But it remained largely a question of degree. The land, according to Scripture, shared in the Fall.

"Hábel was a keper of shepe, & Káin was a tiller of the grounde," the story goes.[20] In the marginal text, the English translators of the Geneva Bible of 1560 assert that, after Cain made an offering of first fruits, God was displeased because Cain "was an hypocrite and ofreed onely for an outwarde shewe without sinceritie of heart." But this claim finds no support in the text itself. Cain's offering is unbidden, wholly voluntary, and precedes that of his brother; therefore, God's response seems capricious. Perhaps God was displeased because Cain—as a tiller of the earth, as one whose sustenance depended on his own labor and ingenuity—had shown a troubling lack of faith in Providence. A shepherd tends to nature's profusion, skims the cream so to speak, but a tiller takes matters into his own hands. To cultivate the soil, then, is the act of an autonomous spirit. What mischief would be beyond such a creature?

> Then the Lord said vnto Káin, Where is Hábel thy brother? Who answered, I canot tel. Am I my brothers keper?[21]

Out of his envy, or his fear, Cain killed his brother and became a fugitive in the land of Nod, which in Hebrew means *wander*.

The terms of these stories dictate that the land be conceived as a living reflection of hope, or of guilt. For minds habituated to attributing souls to things, not least of all to the earth itself, it is not difficult to imagine mountains as object lessons in upheaval and ruin, correlative of violence. "If God created mountains," Nicolson asks, "must they not also be beautiful?"

> But did God create mountains? Were they original with the world, or did they rise at some later period, as a result of human sin, and so remain to man a warning and rebuke, a visible reminder of the sin of man and the wrath of God?[22]

Such a belief, I suppose, belongs to the barbaric myths of a nomadic and prehistoric past. But if you consider the destruction being visited on the earth today, if you consider violence against the land as but one facet of the violence that men inflict on their world—on women, on children, on refugees, on animals—and, furthermore, if you accept the proposition that all of these crimes spring from avarice and fear, from arrogance and ignorance and envy, then the story of Cain and Abel will not seem so strange.

> Againe he said, What hast thou done? the voice of thy brothers blood cryeth vnto me from the grounde.

> Now therefore thou art cursed from the earth, which hathe opened her mouth to receiue thy brothers blood from thy hand.[23]

It's an old curse, this cursing of the earth. "So old," Nicolson writes, "we had forgotten it."

It's sensible to fear mountains, but the plain physical dangers do not account for the terror and hostility they've inspired in Western minds. There are other stories at work, Nicolson writes, in the minds of men who,

> looking at broken rocks and stones on seacoast or among mountains and finding no order, but only wild asymmetry and multifarious confusion, could not persuade themselves that this was the world that the Lord had made and felt themselves rather standing upon the ruins of a broken world.[24]

Luther blamed the fact of mountains on human pride. "The whole face of Nature was changed by that mighty convulsion"; that is, by the Deluge.[25] He was not the first or last to draw a moral lesson from the rocks.

The bus arrived in the afternoon at Leh in Ladakh, where I met a German named Markus. We agreed to hike together over the Shingo La trail, which crossed the Great Himalaya and Zanskar ranges, a distance of one hundred fifty miles. While we stood in the middle of the broad dusty street, making plans for the trek, every shop up and down the street, as if on cue, suddenly downed its shutters. A few hectic moments were succeeded by an eerie quiet as shoppers and shopkeepers vanished. Within seconds, every gate was locked, all blinds were drawn, and all was still. We learned from a passerby that militants had murdered several lamas in a nearby monastery. Within minutes of the arrival of the news, a sympathy strike was declared and the town, as we stood watching, shut itself town.

We divided our food equally and set off.

> Farther east across the glaciers lies the inaccessible country of Zaskar, said to be rich in copper, where the people and cattle live indoors for six months out of the year, where trees are scarce and food is scarcer. (*Imperial Gazetteer*, 1908)[26]

Beside the road, flocks of sheep and goats grazed on sparse grass. The surrounding peaks gleamed with sunlight or vanished in fast-moving squalls. The valley narrowed as the road climbed, and when a passing cloud burst with hail and rain, we sheltered among boulders.

The roar of gunning diesels filled the valley long before the vehicles came into view: two army transports grinding up the road behind us. We flagged down the trucks in hopes of hitching a ride to the head of the trail. The driver of the lead truck, a young soldier with dusty hair, grabbed the submachine gun that lay on the passenger seat and tossed it in the back, and I climbed in. Markus boarded the second.

By gesture and guess we established one another's origins, names, destinations. The young soldier (I'll call him G) seemed to welcome the company. I opened my book to a map of India and he pointed to the state of Kerala, his home state, a strip of coastal land facing the Arabian Sea.

"You're far from home, G," I said.

The soldier laughed. He opened the glove compartment and retrieved a camera that didn't work. I placed batteries from my flashlight into the thing, which appeared to have been dropped several times, but the film would not advance, so he cheerfully threw it out the window. He handed me a photo of himself, with the same unruly hair but dressed in shirt and tie, seated beside a young woman dressed in a sari, who held a baby in her lap. The couple did not smile but gazed soberly out of the photo like a minister's family from Schenectady circa 1840. He considered the photo in my hand and shouted *Far!* and shook his head. The truck lurched up the rubble-strewn switchbacks and the wheel jerked crazily in his grip as we slammed repeatedly into the seats.

The convoy came to a halt in front of a glacier. Four of us stood together in the road, muttering among ourselves, marveling at an immensity as unlikely as the walls of Troy, or a Grand Coulee made of crystal. Great heaps of stone and turned earth lay along the bottom of the glacier's face, like the roots and twigs grubbed up by the Erymanthian boar's snout. The pristine ice was faceted, as a diamond is, to catch the many kinds of mountain light. G, Markus, a Sikh soldier in turban and beard who resembled a Lascar, and I admired the scene with the artless awe of plains people.

At nightfall we arrived at a collection of whitewashed dwellings that bore sheaves of rust-colored barley on the roofs. As the soldiers settled down to rum and cards around a kerosene stove in the bed of a truck, a woman led Markus and me into a wide stall with a low ceiling, where we stretched out on the straw. Markus snuffed the candle stub and we talked in the darkness about war. Markus believed that humankind had not progressed very far, by any meaningful standard, in three thousand years. I disagreed because I was warm and I wasn't hungry anymore and I contended that humanity was fundamentally good.

Markus began to snore. The darkness was the same whether I opened or closed my eyes. The bugs in my clothes began to stir.

We entered a causeway that crossed a vast and stony lake bed compassed by mountains. As we drove, I found no landmarks near enough to confirm that I was, in fact, a body in motion. The truck stormed over the level earth like a wooden ship beating against contrary winds. Corroded obelisks of stone, wasp-waisted megaliths, and twisted stone pillars sprouted in the middle distances.

Somewhere near the center of the lake bed, G's truck blew a tire. After the flat was fixed, we paused to observe a monastery that rose seamlessly from the top of a butte, as though it had been carved from the living rock. No paths could be discerned on the steep cliffsides, and I saw no sign of life

The Sikh soldier said, "Here. Holy men," and drew his finger across his throat.

Here is where the monks were killed.

Looking back along the causeway, it was no longer possible to see the gap through which we had entered the lake bed. Looking ahead, I saw no exit. The mountains had closed in, it seemed, to cut us off.

Somehow, men had crossed snow-covered mountains, clambered up the sheer stone walls, found the monks, shot them, and disappeared.

I wonder how the monks faced their deaths. Was it the moment for which they'd prepared all their lives? Did they die with the composure borne of a lifetime of self-discipline, knowing this life to be but a prelude to eternity? Or did they die like anyone would have, begging for mercy, sobbing in disbelief?

A somberness settled over the place. Clouds sailed over the monastery and brushed the stone with blue shadows. We policed up the tire tools and drove on.

The centuries between Newton and Darwin witnessed a Golden Age of wild speculation. Katherine Brown Collier surveys the unsteady advance of natural philosophy during those years in her book *Cosmogonies of Our Fathers*. The theories she recounts, regarding the formation of the earth and land, are often dizzyingly complex, wholly unverifiable, imaginative flights. Kircher's "panspermia" and Descartes's vortices; the Mundane Egg and the Central Fire. The theories of these men (few women seem to have taken part in this sport) resemble little more than thought exercises, a sort of cosmic puzzle competition. They derided one another's seismological theories and argued the heights to which the waters of the Deluge rose. A surprising point of agreement was the presupposition of an "original fire," the remnant of which presumably still burned inside the earth. This is one of the few instances in which they stumbled into a truth.

Fossils continued to fascinate:

> Antonius Lazarus Moro suggested that fossils were from volcanoes. . . . Hakewill thought that perhaps they were due to demons, who in an attempt to persuade men to idolatry either acted themselves

> or aided men, presumably by the assimilation to real organic remains. Those human agents whom he accused of such activities were princes, who were motivated by a desire for fame, or "*cunning workmen* out of curiosity." Columna, who thought that marine fossils were real, attributed their presence on land to various agencies, including mankind. [Some believed fossils] might have been brought on land by army encampments, by the inhabitants of vanished cities or by monkeys. Columna attributed them to the deluge or to an exchange of land and sea as well as to the casual rubbish heaps of man.[27]

H. Butterfield, in *The Origins of Modern Science* (1949), recounts the old belief that "the fossils on Mount Cenis had been dropped from the food of pilgrims passing that way—fish, for example, that had become petrified in the course of time."[28]

The visions verged on poetry. The German scientist Athanasius Kircher suggested "that the earth was a great distilling furnace with snow-capped mountains for alembics" in which fossils might be formed.[29] That's a pretty image.

Mountains are visionary. See them some winter night: lambent with moonshine, arrayed against the starry sky like a row of votive candles, weightless as paper lanterns. Their peculiar buoyancy was noticed long ago. In a Jewish legend about the first day of creation, it is said that before God made light, the mountains flew like birds over the face of the deep. That's a pretty image, too.

Eiseley suspected that "man has always felt in the presence of great stones and rarefied air something that dwarfed his confidence and set his thoughts to circling—an ice age, perhaps, still not outlived in the human mind."[30]

Positing the interplay of forces was a usual way to resolve difficulties. This method drew on habits familiar to children inventing make-believe worlds and is discoverable in any metaphor (and much humor). Lacking instruments, the cosmogonists combined the materials at hand. The earliest mythologies demonstrate this: the dragon, the mermaid, the unicorn derive from a fish and a woman, a horse and a narwhal, a snake and a bird. The most remarkable feature of our wildest dreams is how mundane they are.

"Leibniz had the idea," Collier notes, "that this globe had once been a sun, and gives a picture of a mother earth solidifying so that its encrusted surface crinkled into mountain-ranges." Anybody can see *that.*

Arthur Koestler, in *The Sleepwalkers*, observes that the "history of cosmic theories . . . may without exaggeration be called a history of collective obsessions and controlled schizophrenias."[31] But disdain for these fantasies would be unhistorical and unkind. There is an adventuresome curiosity, a fearlessness born of unabashed wonder, in these early excursions. Considering the modern estrangement of art from science, not to mention the intensifying specialization within both, we might mourn the passing of an age when a philosopher, a painter, or a playwright felt perfectly welcome to moonlight as a mineralogist.

The cosmogonists had to proceed in the face of centuries of religious dogma that considered the earth as morally polluted. Excessive curiosity was, therefore, morbid. Why should the condemned man measure his prison, or the castaway his island? An inquisitive mind, too, was an overly proud mind. The mysteries of nature had been ordained by the Creator from the foundation of the world, and undue investigations of them were intrusive, presumptuous. "Where wast thou," God asks Job, "when I laid the foundations of the earth? declare, if thou hast understanding."[32] Careless investigators were always open to charges of impiety. Curiosity had led many of the cosmogonists' predecessors to the stake and the rack.

Because speculation about the heavens was less perilous, a wealth of new terrestrial perspectives was generated by the discovery of numberless earthkins among the gigantic stars. The expanding universe revealed new ways by which scientists might theorize indirectly—by the back door, as it were—about this earth. It had been believed that the heavens were immutable, eternally pristine, exempt from the Fall and the Last Judgment, a perpetual visible reminder of earth's degraded nature. Comets were believed to pass below the moon, since such aberrations were unthinkable in the heavens.

But when Galileo observed the spots on the sun, the weightiest distinctions between the sublunary and translunary worlds disappeared: the heavens became, like earth, subject to change. Even the quintessence, the element of the angels, proved susceptible to physical laws. It was becoming more permissible to separate God's punishment from natural processes.

But the eye remained untrained. Voltaire, in a dissertation he wrote for the Academy at Bologna, associated fossils with plain carelessness by claiming

> that they were shells which had been dropped from the hats of pilgrims on their way from the Holy Land to their homes; or that they were shells that had gone astray from cabinets and museums; or, finally, that they were not shells at all, but mere shell-like forms, produced by some occult process of nature in the bowels of the earth.[33]

The idea found its way into his *Philosophical Dictionary*, published in 1764. Goethe responded in his *Autobiography* that Voltaire "only admitted [fossils] as *lusus naturae* [sports of nature]." Voltaire, "in the interest of injuring priestcraft," had injured reason and lowered Goethe's estimation of the philosophe. "These mountains," Goethe wrote testily, "had certainly once been covered with waves—whether before or during the deluge did not concern me."[34]

Scientific discovery cannot have been the sole aim; the theories are too fantastic. Perhaps there is another impulse at work. These men longed to understand but lacked the proper tools, and for this reason they became creators. They put themselves in God's shoes (I wonder if this accounts for the lack of female cosmogonists) and made universes. Their theories are, in this sense, works of art that range from the gaudy to the gorgeous to the comical. As I read their theories, I must remind myself that the stark, flash-lit landscapes they conjured are not far-off, alien worlds, but this one.

Most Europeans, meanwhile, held to the simplest explanation that the creation of the world was revealed to Moses as a reverse prophecy, or series of prophecies—"dark hieroglyphic visions," as Miller calls them—of winged mountains and "pitchy cloud."

How much of our understanding—of the world's origins and of human nature—traces its source to a story, a strange dream, a nightmare from "the times of the Chalk" that some distressed herdsman felt compelled to share with his neighbors?

> . . . when man has performed the most ingenious things, he cannot, save through a cloud, discern what he has done, or what instrument he has used, or what that cause is by which the instrument is moved. (Nicolas Steno, the *Prodromus*)[35]

In 1659, at age twenty-one, Niels Stensen—known to the history of science as Nicolas Steno—made his way out of Copenhagen, a city beset by plague and war, and commenced an itinerant scholar's life among the intellectual capitals of Europe: Amsterdam, Naples, Rome, Vienna. Such a rootless existence was reputable enough in those days, as the life of Erasmus attests. Along the way, he befriended Spinoza, Leibniz, Martin Lister, and other luminaries. He gained fame dissecting horses' eyes, butterflies, the corpses of criminals, and he acquired the feather of notoriety by demonstrating that the heart was a muscle and not, as Descartes had claimed, a furnace. As historian Alan Cutler writes, Steno proved that tears were produced by glands and were not "squeezed out of the brain by the force of grief," which conventional wisdom maintained.[36] He joined the popular pursuit of searching out the seat of the soul, but only long enough to again correct Descartes by discovering nothing supernatural about the pineal gland. (It's unclear to me, by the way, what might have constituted proof of the soul's presence: a burnt socket, a glowing ember, a tiny feather in a thimble of a nest? But that's another matter.)

In 1666, when a great white shark washed ashore at Livorno, the fishermen beat it to death, loaded it onto a cart, and shipped it off to the duke's palace in Florence. There, before the assembled court of

Ferdinando de' Medici, Grand Duke of Tuscany, the young Dane deftly flayed the animal's rotting head.

Steno had seen the animal's teeth before. Most people had. In fossilized form, the sharks' teeth were called *glossopetrae* (tongue stones) and were popularly held to possess magical and medicinal powers. Their resemblance to actual teeth was considered accidental, a "sport of nature." The shark's tooth became a touchstone for Steno's theories about the history of the earth.

In 1669, Steno published an introduction, known as the *Prodromus*, to a dissertation titled *Concerning a solid body enclosed by process of nature within a solid.* He described how sediment suspended in a fluid will sift evenly, over time, to the bottom. A solid, such as a shark's tooth, will maintain its shape as it is buried, and as the surrounding sediment hardens, the tooth will become encased in rock. In this way, he demonstrated how fossils occur in stone, solving the difficulty of *a solid within a solid.* To Agricola's observations on the role of wind and water erosion, which had appeared a century earlier, Steno, in his short work, added his own observations on uplift, faulting, and sedimentation, and in plain language he laid down the principles of modern stratigraphy. His work represented a fundamental insight into earth's history, and the earth's age, that defied the common testimony of the senses. The work was dedicated to his patron, the Duke of Tuscany, Ferdinando de' Medici II.

Evidently aware of the explosive nature of his insights, especially for Scriptural and ecclesiastical authority, Steno opens his dedication with a gentle acknowledgement of the all-too-human aversion to hard truths, our proclivity for wishful thinking. The implicit warning is diplomatically concealed within the broader scientific claim.

He begins with a harmless story, one familiar to most people of that time, and of this one, too.

> Most Serene Grand Duke,
>
> Travelers into unknown realms frequently find, as they hasten on

> over rough mountain paths toward a summit city, that it seems very near to them when they first descry it, whereas manifold turnings may wear even their hope to weariness. For they behold only the nearest peaks, whether heights of hills, or depths of valleys, or levels of plains, far and away surpass their guesses; since by flattering themselves they measure the intervening distances by their desire.[37]

Things are not always as they appear, even—perhaps especially—when you are looking directly at them. "The sea," Steno continued, "was at one time raised above the sand hills, however high."

I imagine Steno standing on an outcrop of stone, gazing across a dry valley from beneath the wide brim of a felt hat. He carries no instruments, for none exist to his purposes. Sandstone cliffs glow pink in the setting sun. The last light of the day dusts the olive trees.

> Before the strata of the sand hills were formed, deep valleys existed in the same places. . . . Where valleys are seen today between the plane summits of the highest mountains, there was at one time a single continuous plain under which huge caverns had been formed before the downfall of the upper strata . . .[38]

The plain corrodes; streams and rivers gouge ever-deepening channels into the land; the remaining high ground collapses. The debris of collapsed ground is swept away by wind and rivers, until all is once more parallel with the horizon, and the still waters begin the slow sifting of their sediment again. Time lapses. "The plane summits of the highest mountains were at one time covered with water."

Taken together, these observations constitute one of the most ramifying intellectual feats in Western history, though centuries would pass before these insights were disseminated, or the implications accepted. As Eoin O'Carroll observed in *The Christian Science Monitor*: "Just as the findings of Copernicus and the astronomers that followed him revealed that the earth is not the hub of the universe, Steno's revolution dislodged humanity from the center of our planet's history."[39]

“Such is the economy of nature that no instance can be produced of her having permitted any one race of her animals to become extinct; of her having formed any link in her great work so weak as to be broken.”[40] Thomas Jefferson wrote these words in 1784. He was an educated man, an enlightened man. I have seen his personal collection of books. A short shelf of them is on display in the Library of Congress in Washington, DC—works of poetry, history, philosophy, science; works in Latin, Greek, English and French. But his understanding of the world was radically flawed. The comforting concept of the *Scala Naturae*—the Ladder of Being, the Great Chain, the Golden Chain, all eternally fixed—which represented the world as Europe knew it, and to which Jefferson subscribed, was soon to be wrecked by Hutton and Lyell.

The discovery of deep time, and the fossil evidence of extinction, raised troubling questions about the human race. If the Creator had indeed made life forms, only to toss them away, what of this our sinful breed? As Eiseley frames the issue, “Why would a supremely rational God reject and repudiate his creations? Furthermore, if such repudiation occurred, was there not danger that man himself might be swept from the stage of life?”[41]

I don’t know how Steno reconciled his theories of geologic transformation with Genesis; I don’t know whether he countenanced the possibility of the extinction of life forms. He never doubted, in his writings at least, the account of the Deluge or the Mosaic chronology. It is hard to believe that the incongruity never intruded on his speculations. Knowledge sufficient to wreck an old conceit—a conceit to which immense power was staked—had come into his hands. At last, he set it aside.

For whatever reason, as the issue became clearer, Steno’s confidence began to weaken. Marjorie Hope Nicolson writes that he was “susceptible . . . to dual moods of optimism and pessimism deeply imbedded in the thinking of his age,” and he never questioned the scriptural promise “that the earth would be destroyed by God.”[42]

Zanskar, Northern India

The mountains appeared passingly through gusts of blowing sand and dust. A whiff of ozone arrived on a thundering wind that whipped spindrift from the snow peaks. In late afternoon, I arrived at a stone hut where an old man sold chocolate and loose cigarettes. I bought noodles and paid for a corner of the room where I could lie down for the night. I did not see Markus; he must have passed during the storm.

In the morning I continued without him. Snowmelt poured from the cliffs at either hand to feed the main stream, where unseen stones knocked about in the current to create a sound like a man beating the earth with a bone.

I came to a place where the trail had collapsed. Hundreds of feet below, the rubble lay slumped at the water's edge. A log served to bridge the gap, but I could not bear to step across, so I slithered out on my stomach. Two hundred feet below, the river heaved and saulted, boiled and crashed. The chasm exhaled a thunderous mist, and I lay belly-down on the log like one suspended in the mouth of a roaring furnace.

Now, seated at the window in a quiet corner on the sixth floor of the downtown library, I watch two hawks kite above the city park across the street. I try to recall the time of day, the precise colors of stone and water, the temperature at that hour, fifteen years earlier, near a river whose name I've forgotten. I am glad that, for once at least, I did not look away. That vision of crashing waters has given comfort to my heart, and it will continue to do so for as long as I live.

Sometimes a memory is like an illicit transaction you happen to witness on a street at night, the knowledge of which makes your life, in some way, a touch more costly, or maybe a few cents cheaper. It depends on who you are, I suppose, and what it was that you saw.

The muleteers sprinted down the trail toward me, shouting and waving, so I turned and ran. We crouched behind an outcropping as skull-sized stones bounded over the trail and plunged off the cliff to the river. The men laughed. The boy tapped my shoulder and pointed to the crest of the hill where three mountain goats stood very still, facing in three different directions, each to his business, each innocent of chicanery. Stones tumbled past, followed by sheets of loose gravel. Forty meters separated us from the next protected section of trail. When the first muleteer ran, the goats marked his progress, turning their heads as one. The next man sprinted, then I did, and the boy was left to guide the mules across the open ground by himself, which he did with admirable and good-natured aplomb—in defiance, I believe, of his cowardly employers.

In a sea of stone appeared a solitary green knob on top of which perched a whitewashed house, and we made our way down to it. Green fields skirted the house, and bronze stacks of barley leaned at the walls. The fields, stepping downhill in crescent-shaped terraces, shone emerald in the cloudlight. I didn't eat or sleep but lay awake in a fever and listened to the small sounds of the goats stalled below.

The men set off in the morning without me. I ate a few spoonful of rice and spinach, thanked the old woman, paid a few rupees, and followed some children a half mile to a spring where I filled my bottle. Then I set off.

After a few miles I stopped at a stone hut by the riverside where carriers and merchants could buy candles and kerosene and rope, noodles and cigarettes. For a day and a half I lay on a bench in the back room, in and out of sleep, with a narrow view of the window where rain clouds alternated with clear skies, and day turned to night and back to day again. It was warm and dry in the blankets, and the salt and chocolate revived me. On the second morning I set off early, dizzy and addled, and the mountains shivered with light.

On Solids was intended as a preliminary dissertation to a great work that would establish the natural history of the earth, but the work, like da Vinci's, was never completed, and the notes Steno assembled have been lost. Cutler writes:[43]

It was in Copenhagen in the winter of 1673 that Steno made his final public appearance as a professional scientist. Dedicating the revamped anatomical theater, he gave an opening statement on the importance of anatomical research. But he now viewed science as simply a way station to more spiritual questions, uttering his famous aphorism:

Beautiful is what we see.
More beautiful is what we understand.
Most beautiful is what we do not comprehend.

Now, with a convert's zeal, he turned his back on science. How to explain this conversion from a lukewarm and accommodating Protestantism to a severe Catholicism? What drove the erstwhile favorite of the Grand Duke's court—fluent in several languages, the renowned physician whose dissections of cadavers drew crowds of illustrious admirers—to the spartan cells of priesthood? What prompted the abandonment of natural science for theology and fanatical self-denial?

Perhaps, in the end, he was glad to trade his scientific inquiries for more abstract devotions, to exchange the rough seas of reason for the still waters of reflection. Maybe it's as simple as that. But I wonder. What isolation, distress, and exhilaration must attend the possession of such insights? Very few people had peered into the age of the earth. To apprehend the rock cycle must have strained his mind and spirit.

He became a priest and requested a posting to the benighted Catholic communities of Hungary and north Germany. In Hamburg and Münster, his rigorous asceticism endeared him to neither the resident clergy nor the congregations. Writing to a friend about his work in Schwerin, he said, "Here the winter has been extremely hard, but souls are colder still, and there seems no way to open them to the warmth of God's love."[44] He begged for alms, foreswore meat and wine, slept on straw, and worked without hope to reform the churches and alleviate the suffering of the poor. "The more one deprives himself of even the necessities of life," he wrote, "the more one accomplishes in the interests of God." Johannes Rose, a friend and convert, recorded that his spiritual and physical exertions left Steno "lean, pale, and emaciated." He suffered anguish over the state of his soul, Cutler writes, and confessed to a friend that he was "living as a dead man who feels nothing." Steno was in a state of despair regarding his pastoral failures, and he wished at times to spend the remainder of his days in penance at some remote monastery.

Instead, his piety earned him the bishopric of Titiopolis, an episcopal see in Asia Minor, in what is now Turkey. An ancient Christian community that had been lost to Islam long before Steno's day, Titiopolis was no more substantial to a bishop in Germany than a fairy kingdom. He regretted the promotion and wished only to serve as "an ordinary priest." Cutler writes that "Steno sold his bishop's ring and silver crucifix and gave away the money. . . . When he wasn't praying and meditating, and when he wasn't too weak from his constant fasting, he tended to his pastoral duties on foot, 'dressed like a pauper.'"[45]

His austerities led to an early death at Schwerin at age forty-eight. Rose's inventory of his friend's earthly estate includes "a wretched black garment, an old tunic, his old cloak, two sackcloth shirts, some small worn handkerchiefs which he also wore as cravats, and a nightcap." His body was returned to Florence at the behest of his Medici friends and patrons.

In 1938, on the tercentennial anniversary of his birth, a modest movement was launched to have Steno canonized for his selfless devotion to the poor. However, positive testimony of a requisite miracle was lacking.

In 1953, as recounted in Raffaello Cioni's book on Steno, Monsignor Giuseppe Capretti (the abbot of San Lorenzo) and Professor Giuseppe Genna (director of the Institute of Anthropology of the University of Florence) received permission from Vatican authorities to examine Steno's remains. As Cioni notes, the meticulous care reflected in the report "would have gratified the scientist. . . . Surely the dissector would not have protested the intrusion." Here is the report filed by the two men:

> The body was found to have largely disintegrated. All that was left were several tufts of hair, distinctly blond in color, and some bones—among them those of the breast and abdominal cavity, the shoulder, the right arm and forearm. The body was covered by a

chasuble, its metal embroidery still distinguishable. Around the head were some small pieces of gold of uncertain origin. . . . The silver embroidery and buttons of a bishop's liturgical shoes could be seen. To the right were found three pieces of the wooden part of an episcopal crozier.[46]

The inscription on the wall of the crypt in the basilica of San Lorenzo reads: "Here lies Niels Stensen, man of God. Born heterodox in Denmark, he was reborn orthodox in Tuscany. . . . He died exhausted from his daily labors for Christ and by his infirmities, to the regret of Schwerin and the sorrow of the Church. Florence wished at least his ashes to be returned to her. Anno 1687." Steno left debts amounting to two hundred thalers, "which he'd borrowed to give to the poor." Cosimo III paid them off.

Steno was denied canonization. He was, however, beatified in 1988 by Pope John Paul II. The date of his beatification was the 5,992nd anniversary of the day that Bishop Ussher (1581–1656) had identified as the first day of creation: the twenty-third day of October of the year 4004 BC.

In the terraced fields, women in scarlet headscarves moved bent at the waist through the waving barley and the roar of water. I dozed on a flat boulder until evening. The Milky Way spanned the sky between the peaks at my head and feet, resembling a footpath bordered by clusters of flowers. To either side of the footpath, meteors darted like fish in black pools. The mountains drew storm clouds from the southern plains, like a lodestone attracts iron filings, and flashes not unlike artillery fire cast the peaks into sudden relief. All night, storms from the plains battered against the mountains.

In the morning, waiting for the sun to reach the path, I sat on a rock and read from the book of Kashmir history. The poet king, it was said, has confiscated the holy manuscripts, lovingly transcribed by the monks, and ceremoniously sunk them in the lake.

A man in a long woolen coat appeared, leading two mules. Young Joe (as his name sounded to me) was a thin, windburned man with a chronic smile. He was headed to Shingo La, he said, tapping the pass on my map, and he accepted some money in exchange for permitting me to tag along. I fastened my pack to one of his mules and we set off. It was good to walk unencumbered, with just a stick and some water. Late in the afternoon, he constructed a shelter from a plastic tarp propped with a short stick, and we crawled in.

During the next day's hike, I noticed movement far below in a valley. The two creatures initially resembled people, but then they cantered and spread enormous wings, lifted from the ground and circled, and rose skyward in flat helixes. Lammergeier. Lamb vultures. The bone-eaters.

The temperature fell, and the mountains receded as we climbed. Shadows rose like floodwaters to submerge the peaks in the evening. Young Joe set up his shelter again and cooked rice and fed his animals. I sat on a stone and watched the stars emerge, feeling out-of-body, listless, unstrung. The constellations foundered on the sharp peaks and sank without a sound.

In the morning, gold light glissaded down the mountainsides as we set off. It may have been past noon when we reached a tract of level ground, but the place was bound in fog and I was unsure if we had reached the top of the pass. Prayer flags, fastened to a cat's cradle of cords, linked the scattered cairns. Young Joe paused to adjust the pack straps.

The sound of tumbling stones was carried off by the streaming mists, and I could hear but not see water rushing over rocks, somewhere near the place I stood. Then the cloud parted and I knelt and reached for the ground, overcome with vertigo, because the mountain had finally arrived. For days I'd walked toward it and it was always *there*, immense but comprehensible, objective, perceptible.

Now it was here, a sheer flight of stone where the sky had been, so close I could smell the melting ice that streamed from its face at a hundred points. The sudden wall soared into mist.

It stayed only a moment, and then the cloud returned, the mountain vanished, and I felt the earth press against my feet again.

Somewhere out of sight, the mule's bells jangled and my knees shook as I followed Young Joe down the path, south toward the highway.

A few years later, I read in a magazine article that, in an incredible feat of labor and ingenuity, the Indian military had laid a road over the Shingo La trail. Now the people of Zanskar no longer have to guide their animals on foot over the pass. I was disappointed that no photographs of the new road accompanied the article. I would have liked to have seen it.

Verdun

The first conversation we ever had, I think, was about a book. *The Tigers Are Burning* chronicled the Germans' summer offensive at Kursk in Russia in the summer of 1943. It surprised me that he'd read it. Before that day, I'd never met anyone who had even heard of the Kursk salient. I had spent so much time alone with books about the Second World War, I was startled to finally find company. John was seventeen and I was eighteen. Of course, we became friends. To find a companion like that is akin to being found, when you hadn't even realized you were lost. In the barracks at the Presidio of Monterey, in 1988, John and I began a conversation about history that hasn't ended, though there have been silences lasting years.

The War in the East was our touchstone. We felt sorry for the Russian conscript: undertrained, underfed, underequipped. In the war's initial stages those men were hurled, with little thought and less remorse, into the teeth of the German advance. Soviet police battalions were deployed to the rear of these hapless, hopeless swarms to prevent their surrender, retreat, or escape, and the conscripts fell by the hundreds of thousands under the enemy guns. They did in fact slow the German advance, if only because it took time, fuel, and ammunition to kill them all.

We marveled at German infantrymen covering forty, forty-five miles per day on foot during those heady, dust-choked, early months—July and August 1941—as the invaders drew ever deeper into the steppe, their routes well posted by burning villages. The infantry divisions merely had to follow, day after day, the tracks of the panzer columns unraveling beneath a featureless, pollen-yellow sky, amid the never-ending sunflowers.

Weeks became months, and sixteen-hour days of marching brought them no nearer to the reeling Russian armies that contrived, somehow, to deny the Germans the decisive victory that would finally bring Stalin to terms. Many German soldiers grew unnerved as each day's march revealed merely more of the same distant, hazy, empty horizon. Many succumbed to the creeping conviction that every mile lessened the likelihood of ever seeing their homes again. For millions, those premonitions proved true.

John and I maintained a tenuous contact over the next thirty years, during which time he served in a war both different and not so different from the ones we'd discussed during hours-long conversations. I visited him in July of 2005, when he was back at the Presidio, at the Defense Language Institute, preparing for another deployment to Iraq. His wife had not yet arrived from Germany to join him, and the two of us sat at the kitchen table and ate steaks and drank cheap red wine. He told me about the bitter fighting in Kufa, Najaf, and Sadr City during the al-Sadr uprising of April 2004. He talked about the insurgents he had killed and the men under his command who had been killed, and I did my best to understand.

I had intended to visit for a few days and then take the train to Nevada. In my pack was a map and a bivouac tent, and I planned to camp in the Ruby Mountains near Elko. Instead, John and I drove together to San Francisco and caught a ball game, where on July Fourth my Reds beat his Giants, and we stayed in the city a few days and drank beer and talked. On the day of my train's departure, at the Amtrak station near the wharf, he offered to take me in his car to the next stop at Truckee, a few hours' drive up the line.

As long as I've known him, John has disliked being alone. He didn't enjoy the thought of going back to the empty house at Monterey. As we drove, he talked about his eighteen years of military service, his family, his duty stations around the globe. The current wars had changed things, he told me. Good people had been killed, friends of his; many capable and experienced officers were dispirited and exhausted, and many others were contemplating early departures from the army. This wounded him because there was nothing in the world he loved more, or was prouder of, than being an army officer. The word *family* does not begin to capture the affection and devotion he felt for the service.

Though it was still several years off, he wondered what a civilian future looked like. After he retired, he said, he might return to California and start a farm. He gladly recalled high school summers spent working in the fields around Oroville, picking vegetables for a few dollars an hour. Or, he said, being fluent in German and Russian, he might get a job with a shipping firm in Hamburg. Maybe go back to school. Maybe manage a casino restaurant in Las Vegas. On the drive to Truckee, we stopped to hike Mount Rose, where we sat on the summit stones and smoked and talked, surrounded by hundreds of miles of empty, dusty horizon.

At night we drank beer on the balcony of a motel. John asked me why I'd gone AWOL in 1990, on the eve of my unit's deployment to the Persian Gulf, and why I decided to return to garrison. I told him that, at the time, I didn't believe that war was justified. I still don't.

But the notion of justification, I'd come to see, was a pretense. I went AWOL, I told him, because I didn't want to die in an oil field.

No one had asked me, before then, why I had run off. His question proceeded from plain, honest friendship, and I've always been grateful to John for that. I told him how I'd gone to see the regimental chaplain to express my objections—how I could not recall what advice the man gave me. One night I just set my ID and dog tags on my bunk and walked out.

It's difficult to gauge my thoughts after so much time has passed, but I believe I knew from the beginning that I would eventually return, that I didn't have the guts to see the thing through. In addition to the fear of death, the thought of someone going to Saudi Arabia in my place was difficult to come to terms with; also, the fear of incarceration weighed on me from the outset. That autumn of 1990, the German papers carried articles about local organizations that were harboring runaway GIs and providing them with food and money. I read these with interest, but such a risk didn't really tempt me. One of those articles quoted an American soldier, interviewed at some hideout in the city, who spoke in idealistic terms of the need for "resistance." He sounded, I recall, like a smart and earnest young man. I felt admiration for his courage, and shame for my lack of the same. Probably, he was caught and sent to prison. I wonder where he is today.

There were other reasons I left. I probably wanted to make the point that I wasn't going to go willingly and would not be rushed into things, which was ridiculous and pathetic, because it didn't matter to anyone if I went or not. I could either go or face the consequences. The army provides a certain amount of rope, and you can either hang yourself with it or not. The choice is yours. It's not a fraternity.

During the drive to Truckee, I told John that I was glad of the decision to return. I wondered once again how my life would have played out if I had persisted in refusing to deploy with my unit. I told John I believed the decision to return enabled me, in the intervening years, to live with myself. John understood, I think—or perhaps, out of kindness, he pretended he did. He said, "Here's the thing: there's principles, and then there's reality. Principles are bullshit, man." But I'm not sure that he believes that.

We arrived at Truckee, ate breakfast at a diner, shook hands at the train station, and parted with too much left unsaid, which is often what happens between John and me.

Nuremberg, the city where I was stationed from 1989 to 1991, had been a reliably friendly town to the Nazi Party. The parade ground of the vast party rallies, made famous by Leni Riefenstahl, was wide as a runway and half as long, and only a block from our barracks. Here, tens of thousands of *Sturmabteilung* (roughly, "assault detachment"), or SA men, gripping silver-headed shovels, gathered in flawless ranks to listen to speeches by Hitler and other dignitaries.

The salad days lasted less than a decade. The winter of 1944 to 1945 witnessed a tough slog by US troops through eastern France and southern Germany, and in January British and American air forces leveled

Nuremberg. The arrival in early spring of US Army scouts at the city's outskirts heralded the end of the grand vision. The massive concrete swastika that crowned the grandstand at the head of the parade ground was blasted by combat engineers at the close of the war, an event that provided iconic newsreel footage of the Allied victory.

By the time I arrived in that city, the parade ground was deserted except for joggers, or couples out for a stroll. It was a peaceful place, and on weekends the nearby ponds and meadows were crowded with sunbathers and picnickers. The great concrete slabs of the grounds were cracked and buckled in places, weeds sprouted in the joints, and trees cast empty shade where the faithful had once gathered to swear fealty to the new dispensation. Four decades after the war's end, Romani wagons were parked here and there at the edge of the parade grounds, half-hidden in the trees.

The barracks installation was built in the thirties, a massive stone and brick affair of five stories surrounded by a high wall topped with barbed wire. Before and during the Second World War, German officer cadets trained there. After the war, the US Army's Second Armored Cavalry Regiment's Command and Control Squadron, along with the regimental engineers, took up residence. C&C squadron was still there when I reported for duty in September 1989, and bullet holes still peppered the arches from the days of liberation. By then, the barracks had earned a dubious reputation among the city's residents. I learned this on my first night in Nuremberg when I went out for a walk, got lost in the rain and dark, hailed a cab, and was surprised that the taxi driver did not know the place by either the German name, *Südkaserne*, or the English name, Merrill Barracks. "Ah, Gangster Hotel," he said at last, and he turned the vehicle around. The phrase was probably among the half dozen in English that he knew.

I paid him and stood awhile on the sidewalk, beyond the gate, surveying my new home. The high walls loomed behind the barbed wire, in a downpour lit by lightning flashes. I approached the guard post with my ID in my hand like a fugitive turning himself in, despondent at the thought of spending the next two and a half years in that place.

Two months later, Berliners hacked through the Wall with pickaxes and we rode in convoy to the Czech border to greet miles-long files of East German–built cars called Trabants, or, more affectionately, *Trabis*. We took pictures and shook hands with East German families and shared chocolate cake and cigarettes. An aluminum pfennig stamped with the hammer and sickle, a token of that day, still sits on my bookshelf. In the coming months, a democratic movement swept through large parts of eastern Europe and central Asia. Even uneducated privates like me could sense that governments and peoples across Europe were being peacefully, and often joyously, overtaken by events.

Eventually, however, the Trabis that lined the streets of Nuremberg departed, war broke out in the Balkans, and within a year we were loading our vehicles onto flatcars bound for Kiel and Hamburg, there to be rolled onto transport ships bound for Southwest Asia. The barracks during those weeks became the site of regular antiwar demonstrations by crowds of Germans blasting music and beating drums, and we had the *unheimlich* experience of being the object of organized and angry protest.

The optimism that broke out in Europe after the fall of the Berlin Wall soon faded, but I will always be grateful for the good fortune to have been in West Germany in the autumn of 1989 when, for a brief time anyway, a belief circulated widely that a just and peaceful future was possible. Perhaps we will witness such a moment again.

Today, the Second Cavalry barracks, once home to Wehrmacht officer cadets, houses the "Federal Department for the Recognition of Foreign Refugees."

In November 1990, when I went AWOL, I spent a few days riding trains around Germany. When I showed up at my friend Petra's apartment, where she lived with her mother, she welcomed me in and praised me for absconding. After a couple days, however, I got restless and anxious, and when I told her I was returning to my unit, she called me a coward. I returned to the barracks at Nuremberg, was docked pay and rank, and was restricted for two weeks to a room in the uninhabited fifth floor of the barracks, where I could think about my choices. I was permitted to visit the chow hall and the chapel and the base library. Pretty light treatment, all in all. My actions incurred the contempt of many in my company. They considered me a coward for trying to dodge the fight, for shirking my duty. It was one of those clarifying moments when you find out who your friends are—moments which occur with merciful infrequency during the span of an average life.

B. and E., two motor-pool mechanics, were some of the few in my unit who didn't hold the AWOL thing against me. They laughed about it and wondered why I didn't have the guts to see the thing through. In their eyes, I half-assed it. Coming back was more pathetic than never leaving at all. Their agreeable indifference to the whole matter, however, was a kindness to me, at a time when such kindness meant a great deal.

Some months later, in a tent somewhere in the Arabian Desert, the company commander, Major Baker, and First Sergeant Ennis pinned my Specialist badge back on my collar, along with an Army Commendation Medal, which is an award I did nothing to deserve. The badge and the medal are to me a reminder of the decency of those two men, and my gratitude for the second chance they offered me.

If you say these sentiments seem altogether confused, pathetic, or misguided, I can only say that I agree.

One day in May 1991 we flew from Dammam, Saudi Arabia, back to Nuremberg after a five-month deployment. Riding the green-painted Bluebird school bus from the airport to the barracks, the soldiers conversed quietly or looked through the windows at buildings, green trees, cars and bicycles, the plate glass of storefronts.

People walking down the sidewalk, people dressed in colorful clothes. How unsettling ordinariness can be, when you stumble into it.

That night, after making the rounds at the bars, B. and E. assaulted two German men on a street downtown. As the Germans' girlfriends kicked the Americans who were punching their boyfriends, I walked away, but the brawl overtook me when some bystanders got involved, and the three of us spent the night in a Polizei station.

B. and E. were not good soldiers, or good people. They drank too much, they picked fights, they did drugs. In the summer after our return from the Gulf, E. often brought his fifteen-year-old girlfriend, along with a bottle of whiskey, into the barracks on Saturday afternoons. He was discharged back to the US, escaping by only a few days a warrant by the German police. B. followed shortly, drummed out for spousal abuse. He bitterly denied the charges.

I saw Petra on a street one night in Nuremberg when I was nearing the end of my enlistment. We hardly recognized one another. Her hair was purple, and I looked, in her words, *wie ein Skelett*. We set off on an aimless walk and found ourselves at the old parade ground, where we walked up and down in the deserted darkness, talking. I thanked her for letting me stay at her mom's apartment when I was AWOL. She told me she'd joined a church and she was learning a new life, learning to cope with depression, working at a new job. It didn't pay much, she said, but it was okay. I told her my enlistment was almost finished, and that I'd given no thought to life after the army. She told me she didn't think much about the future either. It was cold and nearly dawn when we ran out of things to say, shook hands, and said good-bye.

November, 1991

The plane banked over the northern Kentucky hills. From ten thousand feet, the bare trees that covered the snowy hillsides resembled so many fishnets spread on white sand to dry. My godfather, Donald Herman Elsaesser, was at the gate filming the arrivals. I don't know why I did it, but when he called out to me, I told him to put the goddamn thing away. I don't know why I reacted with such meanness. He was a good and generous man, a veteran with difficult memories of a combat tour in Vietnam, and I've always regretted my behavior. He died before I could summon the courage to tell him these things.

I rode back to town with my parents. Beside me in the back seat of the car was a small cooler that contained two lunch-meat sandwiches and two cans of Hudepohl beer. My mom and dad had prepared these things for me.

I drank the beer as the city hove into view, the Cincinnati skyline spliced against a powder-blue sky. The river steamed in the chill air, the coal heaps glittered with sunlight, and snow fringed the banks beneath the bare trees.

We didn't talk much, but it was a glad sort of quiet, and when we stopped at my grandma's, she took my face in her hands and kissed my forehead in the manner of Irish grannies. We drank beer and talked about her childhood in Mayo because she was getting older by then, and to bring up times past was to invite her to a dry, high patch of ground where she could see clearly and far.

Back home, I sat at the kitchen table and read the newspaper. Fighting had broken out in the Balkans again, and soldiers had dragged heavy guns to the top of some mountains to shell some city, but I've forgotten the names of those places. My dad asked me if I needed anything. He told me he was glad I was home, then he put on a hat and went out for a walk. Several young men he had coached and taught in high school, including one who was very dear to him, had been killed in action in Vietnam, and I know thoughts of his former students were in his mind.

There was a lot to say, about these and other things. But it seemed to me that there was plenty of time to say them. More than enough time. Too much time. And at that moment, as I sat reading the paper in the empty kitchen, I felt time pooling at my feet like water.

I don't know what came over me during the weeks that followed, but I stayed away from my home and family. I've searched my mind for the cause, but I find little besides the native stupidity of the twenty-two-year-old male and the restless impatience many soldiers experience after their discharge, when the years of mild suspense and uncertainty are abruptly cut like a string.

After a few weeks, I found myself driving south through Florida in a Pontiac Omega I'd bought for three hundred dollars. On one godforsaken stretch of flat, sunbaked swamp, I heard a rattle and bang and checked the mirror in time to see the Omega's detached muffler bounding down the highway like a berserk, one-legged shorebird from the days before people. The tractor trailer following me executed a smoothly efficient evasive maneuver, barely dodging the muffler. I hit the gas and left the trucker far behind.

I was headed for the Keys, I think, but I don't remember if I got there, or if I turned back at Miami. I don't recall much of that trip at all, or why I went there, or where I stayed. Florida made me nervous. Mere mention of the place, even still, makes me uneasy. I've never been back.

Because I couldn't think of anything else to do, I studied German at the state university in Athens, Ohio. One morning I answered the phone and accepted a long-distance call from the operator. I had not heard from B. for two years, and I had not expected to. I listened to his voice as I stood on the dirty linoleum of the share house where I lived. The call had come at eight in the morning as I was headed out to class, and I had a book bag on my shoulder. I remember the sunlight in the branches outside the window, and my shoes planted on the floor. It occurs to me now that it must have been two or three in the morning where he was, somewhere in Hawaii.

"Man," he said in a voice raspy from laughter or lack of sleep, "I can get you a job in my aunt's bar. You can't believe how fucking beautiful it is here. All you need is a one-way ticket. I got the rest—food, place to stay. It'll be a blast! You never smoked shit like the shit they got here. C'mon, don't be chickenshit. What're you doing anyway? Going to college? *Christ.*"

But I didn't go. I was chickenshit.

If I knew where he was now, I would write him a long letter.

In September 2012, John was stationed in Stuttgart in Germany. I visited him there on my way home from Peace Corps service in Mongolia. During the day, when he and his wife were both at work on the base, I sat on the balcony of the apartment, in the shade of tall trees, and read Alistair Horne's account of the battle at Verdun, *The Price of Glory*.

> Whoever floundered through this morass filled with the shrieking and the dying, whoever shivered in those nights, had passed the last frontier of life, and henceforth bore deep within him the leaden memory of a place that lies between Life and Death, and perhaps beyond either.[1]

This was written in reference to the fighting at Douaumont, one of the Verdun forts that changed hands several times during the battle. When he saw the book I was reading, John suggested we go visit the place. It wasn't very far, he said.

He was granted a three-day pass and we drove into Lorraine, through the mellow sunshine of late summer, past fields of corn and sunflowers, through quiet villages. Sparrows worried the hedges, swallows laced the blue sky, and the birches wore the first touches of autumn. This contested borderland straddling France and Germany (Elsaß-Lothringen in German, Alsace-Lorraine in French) is the region from which my mother's grandparents emigrated to the US. I kept watch for some clue as to why they left, but the peaceful landscape revealed nothing. The hopes and troubles of those years, and the people who shared them, departed with their lives and are now buried in forgotten corners of cemeteries in a dozen Midwest industrial towns.

We visited the Meuse-Argonne battlefield. On the well-tended grounds of the nearby cemetery, fifteen thousand American soldiers are buried. The late-afternoon sunlight grazed the acres of stone crosses and Stars of David, and the stillness was broken only by a stray breeze, or by a burst of sparrows.

John stood amid the rows, hands in pockets, reading an inscription. Four soldiers under his command had been killed fighting in Iraq. Even at a distance, I could see in his posture that his thoughts had returned to those men and those streets.

When I'd visited John in California in 2005, he'd insisted that he never lost a moment of sleep because of the war, and in truth he seemed pretty relaxed, just impatient for his wife to arrive. Seven years later, having recently completed his third tour, he admitted that the aftermath of the first deployment had not been so easy.

Over the following days, he told me of the loneliness of the commanding officer's life, and of the decisions he continually revisits, the life-and-death decisions made hourly during those battles in 2004 when he'd led a company of young soldiers through three months of sustained combat operations. To the disapproval of some of his former comrades, he frankly admires the suicidal courage of the enemy fighters, who died by scores and hundreds battling American tanks, who dashed through fire to retrieve their wounded and were routinely killed in the process. He told me that, if circumstances ever permitted, he would like to sit at a sidewalk café in Baghdad and have a cup of tea with the men who had tried, often with unspeakable valor, to kill him.

We visited some of the small German cemeteries that dot the countryside around Verdun. The cemeteries are still maintained, John tells me, by private civic organizations in Germany. The volunteers, outfitted with garden tools, arrive annually in summer in tourist coaches. But there are signs of growing neglect—overgrown graves, half-toppled fences—and John is saddened by this. The rows of narrow and unadorned plots are topped with *feldgrau* crosses and, here and there, Stars of David. Men of many ranks lay side by side, accorded equal status in death.

We visited the fort at Douaumont, where French and German soldiers fought hand to hand in tunnels beneath the earth. "Each time a heavy shell landed above, lamps blew out, corridors were filled with dust and asphyxiating fumes, and the reverberations underground imparted a sensation of being inside an immense drum," Horne writes.[2] Soldiers, maddened by the heat and noise, removed their masks only to be poisoned by gas.

They died by flamethrower, machine gun, cave-in. Men choked for air even as they were shot and stabbed. A French officer at Verdun addressed his men with these words: "You have a mission of sacrifice; here is a post of honour where they want to attack. Every day you will have casualties, because they will disturb your work. On the day they want to, they will massacre you to the last man, and it is your duty to fall."[3]

The corridors today are damp and lit by dim red lamps hung at long intervals. At a turn where the corridor ends in shadow, I am unnerved, stupidly frightened, suddenly uncertain of the way out. I imagine a *poilu*—a "hairy one," as the French infantryman was known—stepping out of a doorway in a horizon-blue greatcoat, wearing a torn shawl of dust, his eyes rimmed red from smoke.

But the ghosts here are not malevolent. They've had enough of all that. Many combatants naturally came to despise the war and its incompetent prosecutors during those ten months that claimed a million dead, wounded, and missing. Some also came, mysteriously, to form a spiritual bond with the men on the other side, those wretched souls who, alone on this wide earth, knew the horror of the shelling and the mud. In a letter written shortly before his death at Verdun, a German student soldier told his family, "Here we have war, war in its most appalling form, and in our distress we realize the nearness of God."[4]

Survivors recalled how the battle at its height acquired *a life of its own*. How should this be understood? The plan was conceived, the battle was joined, men were baptized in fire: these are just a few ways in which war is figured in generative terms. But what does it mean?

At times I suspect the existence of something hard at the core of each human life, something monstrous and eternal. Not resilient, but uncreated. It is in this refractory nature of life that Verdun reveals a truth too often lost in the immense destruction of humanity that occurred there. A truth that is, in some way, equally sinister.

Imagine a storm of shrapnel, nitrate, and phosgene achieving cyclonic centripetal force, consuming soldiers and machines by the hundreds of thousands. Shreds of daylight whirl like dust devils across the moonscape. Not even a scream escapes, and each man's world is a private Catherine's wheel, furious and thunder-lit.

It may be the battle had a calm, serene eye like a hurricane's, or a gravitational pull like a star. The German physicist Schwarzschild, whose research contributed to the discovery of black holes, was an artilleryman on the Western front during the First World War. Perhaps his experiences played some role in the development of his theories. Do traumatic experiences, such as the Verdun battles, have the power to alter the chemical composition of a human body?

Someday I'll read a book that explains how stars are formed, and there I'll find a clue that reveals how human beings endure the terror we inflict on one another. Stars have long called human beings toward a knowledge of ourselves, and their beauty cannot be merely incidental, the gaudy adornments of some poet's self-consciousness. Their composition and properties—not their brilliance—will yield real insights one day. Or we will continue in blindness to the last day and never mourn the loss of what we never possessed, or what we chose not to know. According to an ancient Greek superstition, to speak in the dark was impious. I think they were afraid it might answer.

After ten months, the battle died. Those who survived Verdun returned to the lines, and many fell in other battles, for the war was far from over. But eventually, the day arrived when a brother or a husband or a son returned his rifle to its rightful owner and made his way home. There, he embraced his mother and father, wife and child. He stowed his kit, ate his favorite meal, told stories, slept. A brother or a son or a husband went home and, to all appearances, resumed the life he had left behind. He moved and laughed in ways familiar to loved ones, he left for work in the morning and came home again in the evening, and as the years passed, most of his neighbors came to forget that he'd ever gone away at all. And late at night when the house slept, and a pair of streetlamps cast the only light in town, he would walk upstairs with a glass of water, sit beside the open window, light a cigarette, and vanish without a trace.

Cycling the Mojave

Sometimes I would talk to my bicycle, or the sky. Just a greeting or an observation, generally. "Hello, moon," I would say on its appearance, or "That was a good ride, wasn't it?" to the bicycle leaning into a bush. Whenever I spoke, my voice would startle me with its intrusiveness, and the words jarred like a casual profanity. In an account of a long sojourn in the Chihuahuan Desert, the author wrote these words about the silence he encountered there: "you perhaps think to break the spell by raising your voice in a cry; but you will not do so again. The sound goes but a little way and then seems to come back to your ear with a suggestion of insanity about it."[1] When I read those words, long after the ride, I knew that nothing John van Dyke could do would ever lessen my affection for him, though he's been dead these hundred years.

I don't know why people take long bicycle rides. There are as many reasons as people who do it. A man in Needles asked me why I was cycling to Flagstaff and I said, without deliberating much, that sometimes I needed to kick the shit out of myself. I was surprised at how readily he understood exactly what I meant, even when I didn't. Sometimes I act without knowing why, but with a kind of faith that the purpose will be made plain in time. But it doesn't pay to examine the issue overmuch because, at the end of the day, so long as I don't hurt anyone, nobody really gives a damn anyway.

Cycling is like that.

California City, California, April

I packed a point-and-click camera, an air pump, a water pack, headlamp, highway map, sleeping bag, a pouch of Drum tobacco, a bivouac tent, two long-sleeve shirts, one sweater, one pair of long underwear, a knit hat; a poncho, rain hat, pencil and notebook; a ditty bag of toiletries; a multipurpose bike tool, a spare tube, and a tin cup; two pairs of socks, two pairs of underwear, electrical tape, binoculars, and a bird guide.

For heating food and water, I had an Esbit stove and thirty heat tabs. One tab heats a pint of water, enough for a cup of oatmeal and a cup of coffee. The Esbit stove is a German product, and it's similar to the one Wehrmacht troops carried into Russia in 1941. The tabs ignite readily in rain and wind.

At Tony's place in California City, laying out my gear on the floor in the spare room, I had to decide what to leave behind. This culling, this commitment to doing without, is both liberating and nauseating. A sleeping mat is nice to have, but you can sleep without one. A paring knife with a plastic handle weighs a fraction of a Swiss Army knife. (I'm not certain, but I would wager that Swiss army soldiers are not issued Swiss Army knives and they don't pedal the Alps with collapsible corkscrews.)

At night Tony and I sat on the porch and talked about family and drank beer. He had recently returned from a yearlong assignment in Afghanistan where he worked as a contractor at a remote base. Guessing that I was feeling restless, and feeling restless himself, he had invited me out to California. He was right, of course: I was restless; most of us are, most of the time. We talked about being middle-aged men without children. We talked about the twenty years that had passed since the army, and the things in life that remained to be done. The things we might have done differently, the places we wished we could return to. He gave me an e-reader as a gift for the ride. That solved a big problem. During past cycling trips I had carried pounds of real books.

I hung around at his place for weeks, because it takes time to work myself up to these things, and because I was nervous about pedaling into the desert. But the day came when I ran out of excuses. We shook hands at the side of the road and I set off.

Mojave Desert

Route 66 east of Barstow winds through several mountain ranges. The Rodman, the Cady, the Bullion, and the Bristol Mountains. The Marble, Clipper, Paiute, and the Old Woman. Mountains ring the horizon, changing color through the day. "Somehow they remind you of a clinched hand with the knuckles turned skyward," van Dyke wrote during his years-long wanderings through the American Southwest at the turn of the twentieth century. In the days when van Dyke wandered the Mojave, the Great Basin, and the Chihuahuan Deserts with his gun, his horse, and his dog, the Colorado River still flowed to the Pacific, the great mining companies had only begun to transfigure the landscape, and gray wolves still roamed the mountains. Those things have changed, but the desert colors he admired have not faded. The land remains painted in the light he described in his book:

> Through the long desert day the sunbeams are wavering skeins of color across the sands, along the sides of the canyons, and about the tops of the mountains. They stain the ledges of copper with turquoise, they burn the buttes to a terra-cotta red, they paint the sands with rose and violet, and they key the air to the hue of the opal.[2]

In the evening, I set up the bivouac tent and read until dark, and in the morning I set off again.

On the third day I reached Roy's Café at Amboy. The water is not potable there, but you can buy it bottled if the place is open. The next place to get a drink is sixty miles down the road. When Route 66 was sidelined by the interstate in the 1950s, its long southerly detour through the desert was cut off like an oxbow lake and began to dry up. The towns along it are ghost towns, or nearly so. Not like the ones in movies, with creaking saloon signs and dust devils, but modern ghost towns: abandoned trailer homes, heaps of scrap metal and building debris, fallen chain link fences, abandoned gas stations with shattered windows, gutted vehicles. Apart from Roy's, a Caltrans repair bay, and a few residents you rarely see, there is little life on 66 between Barstow and Needles. It is a lost highway. The state of California no longer maintains this stretch, a railroad worker told me. The absence of traffic is a boon to cyclists, but the broken surface is hell on spokes, and it's not a convenient place to break down. You'll wait a long time for a ride.

At Essex, a road branches north into the Mojave National Preserve. I sat at the intersection and debated turning onto the road; I'd intended to camp up there a few days. But the ranger station and water were fifty miles away, it was already past noon, and the road disappeared into the imposing Providence Mountains. My nerves failed and I kept straight.

On the fifth day, the wind blew from the east at thirty miles per hour, and I rode the last miles of the Mojave into Needles in a sour mood, feeling discouraged and drained. Outside of town, I found shade and shelter and a thick bed of needles in a stand of wind-warped pinyon pine. Beneath the creaking trunks, in the gusting wind, I fell asleep. When I woke, the wind had grown stronger. I decided then to scratch the trip, get a hotel room, and hitch back to California City. I had cycled the Mojave, I told myself; there's no shame in returning to Tony's place to drink beer on his porch. On the way to town I stopped at an RV park and paid ten dollars for a patch of grass to pitch a tent on, just a few steps from the Colorado.

The river is clear and cold at Needles. van Dyke's Colorado of a hundred years ago was a wild river, but today it flows tamely, broken to the bit of hydroelectric dams. I sat neck-deep in the bank water, looking east to Arizona, where Black Mesa loomed above the blowing sand and dust.

A motel and several RV sites stood back from the river. Rose managed the place and lived in a small room just off the front desk. Pictures of her children hung on the office walls. We talked about the weather. Summer temperatures at Needles reached 125°F and sometimes the town recorded the nation's hottest temperature for the day, she said. But she loved the river.

"Whenever something's going on in my head or I have a bad day, I just go down there and maybe just put my feet in, but that's all I need." She was lucky, she said, to have lived in some beautiful places. "Me and my boyfriend lived in Gatlinburg, Tennessee," she told me. She ran an ice-cream stand there, and her boyfriend worked as a magician for children's parties. "I never really understood him," she said. "I'd wake up and see the mountains all around the trailer and say, 'Look at this place! Look at this place!' and he'd be like, 'So what?' He'd get tired of me saying *Look at this place! Look at this place!*" After a few months, she began to receive threatening visits at her ice-cream stand. "'You need to go back where you came from' they'd say and I'd say 'I'll make a note of that!' and they'd take off, spittin' gravel. Those people poisoned that beautiful place for me. I'd get so angry. I had to leave. I can't be hatin'." So they went to Michigan, where the weather was difficult and people were unhappy. In Michigan, where she worked a cash register, some customers had a habit of paying for items by tossing their coins across the counter, an act she could not tolerate. So they left. Finally, they came to Needles, where the mountains and the river revived her spirits. "'Look at this place!' I said and he's like, *Jesus, not this again.*"

They split up. Where is he now? He must have suffered in the presence of Rose's love of the natural world and her instinctive generosity. His awareness of her rich spiritual gifts must have posed a constant reminder of his lack of the same.

I enjoyed my quiet patch of ground near the water. I paid for three more nights.

At the Saturday farmer's market at Needles's Santa Fe city park, seven stands are set up in the palms' shade. Jewelry and honey, candles and hand-painted postcards and red wine vinegar are for sale. The few older women behind the booths chat with the few shoppers. Along one side of the park is the old municipal government building. The long portico of Greek columns remains, but the structure supporting it is vacant, a maze of bearing walls like a concrete house of cards.

In the neighborhood behind the municipal building, many houses are boarded up. Of the ten motels along Route 66, two are open for business. At the deserted gas station, the numbers on the pumps haven't flipped in years. The old municipal building is the habitation of pigeons now. Not even graffiti graces the place.

Perhaps there is little left in Needles to govern. Rose calls the town's residents "the angry bees" and says the city has given up on development. Meth has ravaged the place, just one of the harbingers of the vast despair creeping across the nation like a shadow. But while Needles fades and frays, the BNSF trains, the Colorado River, and the tractor trailers on I-40 flow through town in their precise and braided streams, uninterrupted, unconcerned, and without cease.

At the city park, men sleep on the grass in the shade of the palms. A handcart containing a plastic bag of clothing stands alone in the sun. Although it is Saturday afternoon, few people are about. At the liquor store, a thin sunburnt woman stands inside the door and informs the waiting customers of the toxic-water lawsuit.

They've been poisoning the groundwater for four years, she announces, and now the lawyers are finally come, just down the street there, so you all better sign up! No one pays her any mind. She vanishes into the sunlight. When I walk out, the wind is blowing heat and dust out of the west, finally in my favor, so I hurry back to the river and pack my things, oil the sprockets, check the chain, and unfold the map I had nearly thrown away.

My hands are shaking. It's ninety-five degrees at 4:00 p.m. on May 5, 2013.

God bless you, Needles! Someday, I'll return here and rent a room on the second floor of some old building, a small room with a view of the town, and I'll sit in a wooden chair beside the window and drink myself to death.

Arizona

On the northern Arizona plateau, dark clouds appeared and the wind picked up. The rain moved fast and caught me in the open. When the rain turned to hail, I pushed the bike into a large drainage pipe beneath the highway. The pipe was about eight feet in diameter, contained a level bed of soft dried mud, and was stoppered at both ends with heaped tumbleweed. Rain clouds lingered into evening, so I decided to spend the night in the pipe. It was cold and confining inside, too dark. Shut away from the sky, it's difficult to sleep. Field rats visited late and their foraging made an outsize sound inside the narrow space. One of them, I believe, made off with a tent stake.

In the morning, I crossed Union Pass east of Laughlin and rode the long decline to Golden Valley, where I met another cycler. He'd pedaled over the pass on a beater bike to visit his son. A gallon water jug was strapped to his handlebars, and a swastika the size of a dinner plate was tattooed on his back. We sat on the curb beside the gas station and smoked cigarettes and talked about bicycles. He told me about his work as a welder, admitted that he was not good at it, and spoke unhappily about the finer points of the trade, of which I understood very little. Then we shook hands and he disappeared. I rode off with dreary thoughts of the miserable, lost, underemployed man with the swastika on his back who had pedaled over a mountain range to visit his child.

A week without a shower is not a crisis. At first you'll be fairly redolent, but exercise, fresh air, and a diet of oatmeal and water will dim the body odor to something more neutral, like stagnant water. After ten days you smell like wet fur. There's a certain level of dirtiness you come to accept, but it's important to observe daily hygiene habits, as you would normally. I brush my teeth and floss after every meal, use baby wipes to clean my face, hands, and crotch. These habits are essential to keeping focused and steering clear of the negative thought pattern, also known as the voice of reason, which tells me that I should be earning money for rent, not pedaling toward Gallup for an appointment with nothing. The reasoning faculty will always talk you out of useless ventures. That's its function. Self-interest is its only interest. Eminently conventional, it always advocates on behalf of common sense. While we pick our ways through the day's petty obstructions, this faculty is interminably calculating the odds, seeking paths of lesser resistance. Also, it is a blessedly reliable identifier of unproductive expenditures of energy, such as cycling.

The negative thought pattern devils me, especially evenings when I am alone in the dark. Mornings, however, are rejuvenating, and I wake at first light and cook oatmeal on my Wehrmacht stove, with half a tab left over for a cup of coffee to warm my hands on. Cross-legged in the sand, shivering in the rising sun, I smoke a roll-up and sit very still and petition Saint Christopher and his beloved Mary for a safe day on the highway.

Route 66, heading east from the Hualapai town of Peach Springs, runs through rolling grassland and juniper groves, and I'm favored by fine weather, little traffic, a tailwind and a good shoulder. At Seligman, where 66 ends, there's no choice but to ride on I-40. It's legal in Arizona to cycle on the interstate, but not enjoyable. Tractor trailers pass at seventy-five miles per hour, within eight feet of one's elbow, endlessly.

As the highway rises and the temperature falls, Humphreys Peak heaves into view, snow-covered at 12,500 feet and obscured by clouds. For four days I camped on Kaibab National Forest land near Williams, twenty miles west of Flagstaff. Afternoons, I kindled a small fire, and only bumblebees disturbed the twilit stillness. There I read about Jakob Boehme's tree of human pain, and how human life is a brief suspension between the earth of our roots and the sky toward which our branches yearn. Boehme's intricate and lovely visions of the moon and the planets, and the correspondences they maintained with earthly life, earned him years of persecution.

The deer visited midmorning. Once, as I sat reading, I felt a slight movement behind me, a suggestion of shifted weight, the merest displacement of a shadow. I turned to see a herd of thirty elk browsing in my direction, forty feet away. Then they got wind of me, and the ground trembled as they bounded off.

Lazuli buntings visited, as did woodpeckers and ravens, each arriving for their allotted shifts throughout the day. The temperature fell as clouds gathered, and thunder rolled through the darkening forest. Evening fell to birdsong, barely audible above the thunder and the rain.

Coyotes wailed. A racket of howls announced a pack moving through the trees, just out of sight, behind some fallen trunks. They were very close. Their strange and overwrought cries were composed equally, it seemed, of torment and joy, a choir of struck nerves followed by a sudden quiet. The birds sang, and nothing moved in the trees.

Boehme says nature is the signature of God or, alternately, a parable about God, who manifests himself within men and women. God is also the "author" of nature, so that a vigilant seeker, looking on the world with the eyes of the heart, might discover God's works reflected in herself—might see herself truly, that is, her blood relation with all of creation.

"God in all things and all things in God" was a critical insight among the Radical Reformers in those years. They were mostly German and Dutch and English, and their activity corresponded historically with the early years of the French Enlightenment. The reformers rejected equally the legalism of the Catholic church and Luther's intolerant reaction. They were despised by both Protestants and Catholics, persecuted and banished and burned. But their doctrine was never entirely extinguished.

God in all things and all things in God.

Snowcapped Mount Agassiz falls behind and the land opens up in the Painted Desert north of Flagstaff. The infusion of light and heat from the unrestricted sky, after days in the forest, is liberating, and pedaling is easy. Solitary blue buttes shape the horizon.

There's a section of Route 89 where the highway narrows and the shoulder disappears, so I hitch a ride with a man in a pickup. He shoves a bale of straw to the corner of the truck bed and I lift the bike in. As we set off, I ask if he's a farmer. "Sort of," he says, slipping a cassette into the player. "I'm a sheepherder." The music is voice and drums, and he sings along. When I ask what the words mean, he says it's not words, it's Navajo traveling music.

The bronze cliffs rise higher and edge nearer. "No one knows what the cause of the problem is," he says, turning the volume down. "Democrats, Republicans, everybody blaming each other. But tell me this, whose face is on the penny? That's right, Abraham Lincoln. Lincoln's face is on the penny. That's the problem." He pulls over before I can think of a sensible response. I stick out a thumb again.

The next car to stop is an aging compact with a bike rack and three men inside. The driver takes a good deal of time and care to secure my bike to the roof. The other two men are journalists for a magazine, here to do a story about Chip, the driver, who is an artist from North Carolina. He has lived on the reservation for many years, and he is taking the journalists on a tour of his work.

A thin man with glasses and a beard, Chip continually scans the passing desert as he drives. His work involves taking photographs and superimposing the images onto the walls of houses or roadside jewelry stands or water tanks. The wall of one such stand, south of Bitter Spring, bears a sample of his work: an image of a shepherd following a file of sheep up a rocky path. The women at the stand—an older woman wearing a scarlet headscarf and a younger woman with a child—are not strangers. Chip has met them before, and they chat in the shade about mutual acquaintances while the journalists photograph the work.

Chip and the journalists prepare to head back to his place, and as we take the bike down, he asks me if I need any water. "Be good out there," he says, and they drive away in a funnel of dust. I wonder about him as I pedal off. He gave me the uncommon impression of a soul at home in the world, though he was on some counts a stranger in this place. His passion is making art from life on the reservation, then imposing the images on sun-faded wooden walls along lonely desert roads. What strange things people do!

When he came to this place years ago—an artist, a doctor, a Black man, an easterner—I imagine he thought a good deal about the mystery that dwells at the unnamed core of every being, which some call *identity*, for it is this subject that lies at the heart of his works.

By now, I'm certain, after all these years, Chip has arrived at a few insights about us.

There is a great struggle underway, a war that is being waged between, on the one hand, greed in its multitudinous and protean manifestations, deeply invested in its own apparent innocuousness, practiced in the arts of mendacity and diversion, celebrated as the American way; and, on the other hand, Chip (along with a small troop of fellow travelers). At stake is the integrity of the individual soul. In its preservation lies our only hope. Once lost, it will not be regained, though some will make a lot of money.

After Chip left, I talked with the older woman. She'd learned English at a mission school near Los Angeles and traveled over the years, she said, to New Mexico and North Dakota and many places in between. I asked her about the road ahead. She told me it was a long uphill ride to the next available water, but then it was all downhill.

Four hundred feet beneath Navajo Bridge, the Colorado turns through Marble Canyon. Its whorled surface gleams like slate after rain, and I hold my hands out to the cool air wafting up from the depths. John Wesley Powell, one-armed Union veteran, was the first white man to raft the length of the Colorado. Very little escaped Powell's attention, and he was an astute and creative observer of nature. One evening by the fire, on the banks of the roaring water, as he smoked his pipe and waited for the coffee to boil, Powell took a moment to pen this curious impression of meteorological conditions on the river:

> Clouds creep out of canyons and wind into other canyons. The heavens seem to be alive, not moving as move the heavens over a plain, in one direction with the wind, but following the multiplied courses of these gorges. In this manner the little clouds seem to be individualized, to have wills and souls of their own, and to be going on diverse errands—a vast assemblage of self-willed clouds, faring here and there, intent upon purposes hidden in their own breasts.[3]

As the weeks passed and provisions dwindled or were lost to rapids and mishaps, the canyon walls rose steadily until the men floated thousands of feet beneath the canyon's rim, which is to say, thousands of feet beneath the level, sunlit earth. The sky was reduced to a narrow strip directly overhead, and the strip alternated red, blue, and black: morning, noon, and night. Three men of the party lost their nerve in those depths, which grew deeper by the hour, and from which escape seemed increasingly improbable. They despaired of ever emerging from the canyon and decided to climb out. Powell, being a scientific man, knew there was an end to the canyon, as there is an end to all things in this world, and he decided to press on. There were no recriminations between the two parties, but tearful farewells and prayers of Godspeed, in what must be one of the most poignant moments in the history of exploration.

The three men succeeded in climbing out of the canyon, but on the way to the nearest Mormon settlements they were mistaken for fugitive white murderers (who, by a stroke of bad luck, were in fact at large at the time) and killed by Indians. Powell and his diminished party completed the voyage, successfully charting the entire course of the Colorado. Years later, Powell met some of the Indians who were involved in the killing of his former companions, but there was no confrontation, no demand for restitution—only a mutual and philosophical acceptance of life's harsh contingencies.

I camped below the Vermilion Cliffs. In the morning, for the first time in two weeks, I set off with the rising sun at my back. A day's climb brought me to the cool pine forests of the Kaibab Plateau.

There are many things to do before I die. I have to learn basic geology. I have to read the works of the madman Paracelsus, also known as Theophrastus Bombastus von Hohenheim, who said that all he knew about life came from the midwife and the hangman. I want to study Hinduism, learn to read Latin. I have to visit the Andes Mountains, South Africa, and Idaho.

There isn't much time. I've wasted many days, which I am perfectly free to do. The body is bound to death, but freedom is unaccounted for, and may even be a lie; it engenders hopes that cannot be fulfilled and conjures dreams that cannot be attained, until the heart breaks under the weight of perpetual disappointment.

The freedom of the human will is mysterious. It's like this: the Old Watchmaker has made a watch, it's true, but the watch, by some sorcery, has contrived to transform itself into a music box. Worse, a music box with ambitions.

The road from Colorado City to Hurricane is a long and steep decline with no shoulder, and I took blind curves at thirty-five or forty miles per hour to keep ahead of the truck traffic that I knew was closing fast. I was sweating and shaking when I rolled onto Main Street. The seat bracket bolt broke on the way down and I couldn't find the part in town, so I thumbed a ride with a man driving an RV to St. George.

Tom was a retired New York City policeman, recently separated from his wife, driving alone from park to national park on his way to Zion. He kept a conversation with me from the rearview mirror as I sat behind him, holding onto my bicycle. He told me about his years as a cop, the frequent ugliness of it, and the recent storm in New Jersey that had left many of his neighbors homeless. The big Western sky and the desert vistas were therapy, he told me, and we talked about the healing properties of mountains. He grew quiet, wiped his eyes, and apologized.

We pulled into the lot of a Utah Department of Transportation facility and Tom entered the open bay with a warmhearted greeting for the workers, who responded with genial surprise to the intrusion. His good nature disarmed the place. Soon, four men and women were standing around my bike, examining the broken bracket, searching tool cabinets for washers and bolts. Within a few minutes the seat was repaired, and I parted from Tom in the sandy lot. As we shook hands, I asked him to tell me Rabbi Hillel's words again, so I would not forget.

I pedaled off in high spirits, struck by the generosity and decency of strangers. At midday the wind blew hot and contrary, so I quit riding, lay beneath a cedar bush, and slept.

If I am not for others, what am I?

In Veyo I found a gas station with an attached shower stall and washed for the first time in fifteen days. Outside of town I stopped at a house to ask whether the land nearby was Bureau of Land Management (BLM) land. I told the woman about the generous people I'd met, and she smiled at a piece of good news. In a thousand years, she said, when people recognize the world for the beautiful place it is, the earth will be a paradise again. This future paradise, she continued, was a real event that would occur in real time, for every human being and for every living thing.

She told me this with a glad and startling confidence, then asked me to wait, and she disappeared around the back of the house, leaving me in the garden among the cacti and the sheet-iron flowers embossed with seashells and broken glass, whose petals were frayed to black by the flame of an acetylene torch. She returned with a mason jar of homegrown tomatoes, refused payment, waved off my gratitude, and directed me to some public land down the road where I could pitch a tent. In the desert that evening, as the sun set behind the cliffs, I ate the tomatoes with chunks of bread. It was good.

A year later, as I read a book about John Bradford, an English reformer who preached the heretical doctrine that all living creatures—plants and animals and people—would one day be freed from death and restored to life in Paradise, I recalled the words of the woman in Veyo. And several years after that, I met Judith Carpenter, an English woman from Newcastle, who at the age of sixty-seven carried a rucksack nearly as big as herself from Saint Jean Pied de Port in France to Santiago de Compostela. One day on the Camino, Judith reiterated to me the same vision of a new earth, which was precisely this earth. She used the same words that Bradford used, and spoke with the same cheerful confidence as the woman in Veyo.

Foolishness, perhaps, but a holy foolishness, and I must never forget what these people have said to me, not a single word of it. Such madness sustains life, no less than bread and tomatoes, and maybe more so.

"Nevada's a tough bastard," the old man said as I pulled up beside him. We were at the Utah-Nevada border, on the shoulder of the road. I was heading west, facing the long downhill from the cool green Utah plateau to the Nevada desert at Panaca. Gene was headed east. He had started in Riverside and was headed to Maryland. On his bicycle was a handmade sign bearing the name of the foundation that was raising money for research into the causes, and a potential cure, for a rare condition that was presently ravaging his daughter's health.

"There ain't nothing there! The wind's constantly in your face. No water for long, long stretches. Nothing." His were the look and the voice of discouragement. His bike seemed a bit overloaded to me, but I didn't say anything about it. A small red plastic pennant waved from a ten-foot whip antenna fastened to his bike's rear rack. It seemed an odd precaution for a man without a helmet. His face, arms, and legs were peeling, flea-bitten, pinpointed with scabs, bared to the sun and wind. Gene was seventy-one years old. In addition to raising awareness of a vicious and little-known disease, he aimed to become the oldest person to ride a bicycle from coast to coast, "solo and unsupported," as he said.

I opened my map and he showed me places in Nevada where I might fill my water bottles. Distances between water sources, he explained, at times exceeded a hundred miles. He pointed out the mountain passes I was to cross, eleven in all. "It gets old. Nevada's a tough bastard. You know," he said, "there's a difference between youth and old age. I know that now." I wished him luck and coasted down toward Panaca, toward the mountains ranged along the western horizon. I don't know if Gene completed his trip. I hope he did. I like to think his spirits revived in the fresh, cool Kaibab, where water was never too far away.

The eleven mountain chains across Nevada, between Utah and California, are more or less a day's ride apart. After pedaling from one range to the next, I arrived each afternoon near a summit pass, where I camped among the junipers.

Rachel, Nevada

My seat bracket bolt had broken again. Sarah, the diner's waitress, told me of a man in town who owned a dozen spare bicycles, and she offered to drive me to his place. On the way, speeding past trailers that lined the wide dirt lanes, she told me that the man's partner had hanged herself only a few months before. "Right there," she said, pointing to a sun-varnished shed knocked together from sheet metal.

"He likes his whiskey more than his beer," Sarah told me. "You can tell he ain't got any family. He broke down on the highway two years ago and we towed his truck here and he never left. I think he's got a couple boys somewhere, but they don't visit."

I said the booze helps a person forget. "Yeah," she said, drinking a can of Coors, smiling to herself. "But you always wake up. He ain't allowed in the diner anymore. Drinks too much. Roger! Hey, Rog!"

Roger was feeding chickens when Sarah and I found him. He lived in a compound of broken trailers, lean-tos, sheds spilling car parts. Tall, blue-eyed, broad-shouldered, he must have been quite handsome once, but all that remained of his youthful health was an afterimage, a hint in the trace of his jawline, a suggestion in the tilt of his head. He greeted us with the self-conscious solicitude of the lonely man. He led me to the bicycles that leaned four-deep against the wall of a wooden shed. We quickly found a bracket that matched, and he picked up a hand sledge and hammered at the old bike's seat, which had seized fast with rust. He hammered furiously, began to sweat, and finally knocked the thing free. Together we rooted through the shed and found the proper bolts and washers. Sweat dripping from his nose, he bored wider bolt holes in the bracket. The new bracket fit snug, and I slipped the seat on and asked him what I owed.

"A twelve-pack would be all right," he said.

At the diner that afternoon, I ordered a Coke and talked with the waitresses. You have to do without some things, Carol told me, if you live in this town. The nearest school, where their kids go, is fifty miles away. But they like the heat, the quiet nights, the desert. Each of them had lived in Las Vegas at some time in their lives but, they told me, people generally come back.

The waitresses in Rachel; the prosperous Mormons of Colorado City; the sheepherding Navajos of the Painted Desert: the United States is a various place. We are referred to by politicians as "the American people" as though we shared a common culture and history, but I don't believe it.

If the Catholic, beer-drinking Reds fans of Cincinnati's west side and the ranchers of southern Utah were to encounter one another, I imagine they would find little to converse about. Each would be in a hurry to get away. "American" is a political label that pertains to passports and not much else, as far as I can tell.

Carol gave me the key to the shower room and a clean towel; Sarah took my dirty clothes and set a cold beer in front of me. I hadn't asked, and they would take no money. "We like helping people who ain't greedy," Carol said. If she knew the truth, I thought, she'd gladly watch me starve.

I sat in the shade at a picnic table and smoked a roll-up and caught up on my notes, and soon enough it was too late to ride. Sarah showed me to a grassy strip behind the diner where I could pitch my tent. I spent the remainder of the evening reading as the mountains changed color, pausing to admire the resourceful precision of sparrows nipping sizzling bug parts from the radiators of patrons' cars.

By now I'm trimmed down to essentials. My gear and bicycle are tested and proven durable. I have confidence in them, and this confidence is liberating. With a few packs of oatmeal, some peanuts and raisins, some dehydrated milk, and a few liters of water, I head out of Rachel at dawn. Mechanical difficulties—broken seat bracket, broken spokes, punctured tubes—have been met and dealt with. The negative thought pattern has vanished. I dwell less, observe more, sleep enough.

The cries of coyotes mingle with dreams through the freezing, predawn hours. But the sun rises and warms my hands and face. As gratitude becomes habitual, I've discovered, weariness diminishes. Discipline is a source of self-reinforcing energy, but it requires all the powers of attention merely to remember this.

Tonopah, Nevada

There's a used bookstore in this mountain mining town. The owner told me she had just finished a book about a man who rowed alone across the Atlantic Ocean, and we wondered at the lunacy of some folks. On the philosophy shelves I found Thomas Merton's *The Monastic Journey* and bought it for $1.25. Along with the paperback, she handed me a homemade cookie "for the road."

From the edge of town, I looked down into the valley where US 6 was buried in the dust of a windstorm. The wind blew cold at forty miles per hour, and the air, even on the mountaintop at Tonopah, was freighted with sand. Far below, the desert brimmed with dust as Alpine valleys brim with fog. The desert floor was a cauldron ringed with mountain ranges, a sea of dust the color of blood in water. I tied a bandanna around my face like a stickup man and set off downhill. The temperature dropped with the visibility. The desert appeared briefly between blowing curtains of grit, and the tractor trailers grinding uphill out of the storm were tall shadows punctuated with the brief gold slashes of high beams.

When I'm seated by the roadside resting my back, a driver will sometimes stop to ask if everything's okay. If I'm walking the bike the last few miles to a summit pass, someone will stop to offer water or a candy bar.

When a spoke broke and I had to thumb to the nearest town to find a bike-repair shop, people stopped: a woman who cooked lunch for the miners at Medona; a retired Las Vegas cop with a pistol and clips of ammunition on the dash of his truck; an auto mechanic from Williams, Arizona, with his young son, driving a wrecker to Flagstaff; an over-the-road trucker from Kentucky driving a car trailer to Oregon; a retired couple from Santa Monica who drove far out of their way to assist me; a Navajo woman on her way to work at a tribal police station; a couple in Benton, California, who offered me a bed in the trailer behind their home. They were from cities and farms; they were men and women; they were white, Black, and brown.

If I were Black or brown, of course, I would not have benefitted from such kindness. Cruelty, and theft: the incalculable, colossal theft of human freedom and human possibility. Myself, the trafficker in stolen goods.

The bicycle, too, induced much of this good will. A person on a bike cuts a harmless figure. The big clumsy helmet is as disarming as a red Geneva cross. Cycling is a pacific activity and seems somewhat silly to the average person behind the wheel. A cyclist is approachable, especially if they are alone fifty miles from the nearest crossroads. I think, people just feel a little sorry.

It's a fact that most people are on the lookout for someone to be kind to. This may be in answer to some unconscious suspicion that existence is justified, in some way, by small acts of selflessness. But much faith is required to accept the proposition that goodness is instinctive. The world belies that notion every day, in a million ways, and mocks it endlessly. To confess that sort of faith is to invite derision; to act on it is seditious, if not plain batty. Still, the fact remains.

Nevada 375

Once an hour or so, a vehicle passes. Tumbleweeds bound across the empty highway, and the wind roars like the sea. At midmorning, as the heat gathers, whirlwinds begin their rounds and devils of chalk dust spin across the dry lake beds. The devils lean into the wind, funnels draining silence from heat, aimless and mesmerizing as spun nickels.

A pair of F-16s banks low over the desert, five hundred feet off the ground. With a dip of their wings, they sling across the cliff face and ricochet into the deep gray sky. The memory of their passage, like a distant avalanche, rolls among the mountains long after they've gone.

The road leads through canyons, over mountain passes, past dilapidated corrals. Cattle wander the rabbit scrub and startle when they see me. US 50 in Nevada is called "The Loneliest Road in America"; Nevada DOT signs say it's so. But I believe NV 375 is lonelier. Like the oxygen of a different planet, the stillness of the Great Basin is wearying. The yips and howls of coyotes arrive on the wind, out of the empty desert.

Then, around noon, this thing happens: a powerful tailwind arrives to sweep me along, up and down the long valleys, and I pedal only to maintain balance. Sometimes I pull onto the shoulder and it's like stepping off a hurtling train. I sit on a stone and smoke a cigarette, feeling addled and unstrung, like somebody who's just walked out of the sea. So I climb on the bike again and I'm carried along at thirty, thirty-five, forty miles an hour, until I no longer hear the wind but am borne along inside it, so to speak. There are moments during a long ride when the wind and the land conspire to speed you across mountain ranges. These are the rare, good times.

I set up the tent at a summit pass at 6,500 feet. The horizon line, broken by ranges, runs for a hundred miles around the center point of my stone seat, and within its compass I see nothing stirring. Daylight fades. I boil water for coffee and my hands shake.

Separation, division, exile: people from nature, purpose from people, people from people, individuals from themselves. In the paradoxical way of things, increased fragmentation does not result in increased autonomy for the fragment, but increased isolation. Thus do prisons of many kinds multiply, and there is immense profit in their proliferation.

Only free people overcome fear. Here again is the awful intuition of the old religions: how atonement liberates, and fortifies, the spirit. Augustine, in Book II of the *Confessions*, thanked his Lord for the strength to recall pain without fear, knowing that such strength accrues to the forgiver and the forgiven alike. As one scholar observed, in a commentary on the bishop's works, "memory without fear is the fruit of forgiveness."[4]

But this forgiveness, for oneself and for the world, must proceed from a broken heart; a broken heart is the alembic in which compassion is quickened. This is why, in the old story, a man of sorrows came looking for other men and women of sorrows, and forgave precisely those who loved too much. Brokenheartedness is a discipline learned in shame, in failure, and in years. Forgiveness is, in this sense, a homely art, self-taught for the most part. It has a power to destroy power, and to make free. Human freedom is precipitated by this strange alchemy. I've read about it in books, I've seen it practiced. This is the truth that sets free. But this truth is beyond me, every day.

Nevertheless! In the moment I stop believing it, I hope I have the courage, as Judas did, to hang myself.

The struggle to become a free and creative person will nearly always end in failure, because I am compounded of spirit and clay, forever drawn upward and dragged down. This bipolarity is a torment and represents a struggle that is unending. Unending, but not hopeless.

The struggle between body and spirit is realized in the desert. The desert is where there are no excuses anymore, where there is nowhere left to hide. In Exodus, the people's desert sojourn lasted two generations, and there they encountered the living projections of their deepest fears.

> There were the hairy satyr (*sair*), the storm devil (*shed*), the howling dragon and monster (*tan*, *tannin*), the winged female night monster (*lilith*) . . . and the collective figure for all the desert spirits, Azazel.[5]

They followed a towering cloud of dust and smoke by day, not knowing where they were being led, and at night the cloud became a soaring pillar of fire, and there was little rest, because the twin columns of smoke and fire did not subside. The people resented a rootless exile that lasted years and promised no end to suffering. Who wants to be deprived of comfort or security? In Egypt, their servitude had by no means precluded happiness. In Egypt their numbers grew and the people thrived. When the call came, it did not meet with great enthusiasm.

John Jackson, member of the sect of Radical Reformers known in seventeenth century England as Seekers, wrote that "in this desart he kept thee the longer to acquaint thee with the disposition of thine own heart."[6] In this desert of hard truths, I am bound to find my heart ill-disposed. But sooner or later, I must come to this place of reckoning, where I will be confronted with my self, stripped of all pretense, my prejudices proven malevolent, my habits lazy and foolish, my capacity for self-delusion bottomless, and then there will be no more turning away.

After four weeks I cross Montgomery Pass near Boundary Peak and enter California again. New birds appear. From the Raven Realm of the Mojave, through the Grackle Lands of the northern Arizona plateau, I now enter magpie territory. The changing ranges of birds, more than anything else, tell of distances covered. They are, perhaps, the only political divisions of any lasting interest.

After the ride across Nevada, I rest for a few days near Bishop. From the campsite I can look south along the eastern slope of the Sierras. Over the horizon are the towns of Big Pine and Lone Pine and the canyons at Red Rock, and beyond these lies the Mojave, where the land opens out again, where solitary mesas rise in perspective haze, and where the canted pillars of familiar dust spin. California City is down there, and my good friend Tony. I look forward to seeing him again.

In Benton, I sit on a bench outside the library, riveted by the greenness of things, by pines and flowering bushes in abundance. This fresh and vivid life is a tonic to the eyes, a good medicine. A woman named Anne stops to ask me where I'm headed. She offers me a place to stay for the night.

Anne and her husband Walt offer the use of their shower and washing machine. In the evening Anne plays piano, rehearsing for an upcoming performance by the community choir. Walt and I bring our drinks out back to watch the moon rise over the White Mountains, and we talk about books as evening falls.

In the morning there is hot coffee and a chat beside the kitchen window, and the three of us watch rabbits sip dew in the grass. Blackbirds, California quail, and phoebes visit the backyard feeders as Walt cooks breakfast. After we clear the table, they give me a new map and a set of panniers to replace the frayed backpack I've been tying with cords to the bike's rear rack. Now, Walt says, "you look a little less H.O.B." Homeless on bicycle.

When I'm packed and ready to leave, I tell them their kindness is currency to me, and I feel foolish as I promise them that I will try to spend it wisely. As I turn out of the driveway, they stand arm in arm on the porch, smiling and waving.

The Western Terminus

Gansu Province lies in northwestern China, on the Mongolian border, between the ice-capped Qilian Mountains and the Gobi Desert. When traveling by train in this region, long tunnels break the journey into discrete landscapes, each unlike the previous. China's new bullet trains reach 140 miles per hour, and to move at speed through this land is akin to turning the pages of a desert atlas, or an itinerary of "Attractions" compiled by the Foreigners Bureau of some gas-rich, central Asian dukedom, freshly semi-autonomous and snowbound eight months a year.

Scenes pass in swift succession: high-rises of glass reflecting distant snowy ridges; cooling towers smoldering in a gray grove of smokestacks; a defunct coal plant of stalled conveyor belts and brick piles.

Blue-black clouds brood over a half-built town of trashed causeways and littered irrigation ditches. A small city shrugs against the base of a mountain range; another lies jumbled on the open plain, as though it's been swept there by an enormous broom.

Golden minarets stand sentinel at a mosque built in pagoda style, and herds of horses browse in the emerald grasslands that lap the foothills of the Qilian.

A white nomad's tent, deep in the green steppe, is staked in the shadow of blue peaks. Whelmed by mountain distances, the solitary little habitation is still enough to draw the eye. From a human perspective, a small human presence has a way of counterpoising immensity.

Many thanks to Hongying Zhang for her assistance in editing this final essay.

Outside the industrial town of Jiayuguan is the mud-brick tower called First Beacon, the western terminus of the Great Wall. For caravans bound for Persia and points west, this was the last place to rest and refit. Conversely, for merchants emerging from the steppes of present-day Turkmenistan and Uzbekistan, this tower betokened one's return to the Middle Kingdom.

First Beacon served as an observation tower. A signal fire ignited on the platform would have been seen by the next beacon, miles to the east, where a ready pile of tinder would be lit. The American translator Red Pine recounts that these towers "burned straw at night and wolf dung, which emitted an intense black smoke, during the day."[1] By these means, an alarm could be transmitted a thousand kilometers in a few hours.

Soldiers posted to this section of the Wall were not expected to repel an attack; the place was thinly manned and too remote to hope for timely reinforcement. No, this was tripwire duty. The primary task of each small and isolated garrison was to alert the nearest command before being overrun. To sound the alarm and stand their posts: that was the mission.

From First Beacon, perched on the rim of the Taolaihe River canyon, the view is essentially the same today as it would have been for the T'ang-era conscript serving his shift of guard duty on a summer day a thousand years ago. The sky above the peaks is a changeable array of gray clouds that part at times to reveal the violet, high desert sky. To the north are the Black Mountains, and the southernmost reaches of the Gobi, which stretches over a thousand kilometers north to the Altai Mountains in Mongolia.

In the days of the T'ang empire, conscripts were compelled to serve one year of border duty, and the young man who had the misfortune to be assigned to the First Beacon sector could anticipate long vigils exposed to arctic winds in winter, blistering summer heat, and spring sandstorms barreling out the Gobi that blinded the sun. Then as now, the days turned fire-orange with blowing dust that caused grievous eye infections among people and animals.

Then as now, wolves prowled in packs. Loneliness, fear, and the hopelessness of such a position would have preyed on less-sanguine minds, piling imagined threats on real ones. Weeks, months might pass without sight of a human being, a stillness disturbed only by a fox or a noisy flock of geese. But the enemy was there, near and unseen, their presence betrayed by an unaccountable column of smoke beyond the ridge, or by hoofprints in the morning frost, which vanished with the rising sun.

This afternoon, however, all's quiet in the First Beacon sector. The enemy moved west long ago. A blue cloud sails down a high slope, leaving a narrow blanket of snow like a snail-track in its wake.

At Saint James Elementary School, the history of China was covered in a few paragraphs. Two facts from that lesson have remained with me to this day, and both pertain to the Great Wall. At its western extremity, the text asserted, the Wall was made entirely from sand, while at high altitudes it was built of compacted blocks of snow. Although the claim may have contained more imaginative than material truth, I could imagine, in vivid detail, men in leather helmets and long moustaches stacking blocks of snow along an icy ridge, or building a sand castle that could house a hundred armed men and their horses.

I carried the images with me for forty years, and I recalled them as I stood at the base of First Beacon and rested a hand on a course of bricks made of sand and mud and straw. In that moment, a marvelous outlandish dream from a sixth grade social studies text became real. But I was no longer a child, and the sand of the ancient bricks turned to dust at the touch of a finger, and I sensed the presence of a timeless sorrow laced with futility and with suffering, a sorrow that nevertheless refuses, despite its forlornness, to be forgotten.

Death-remembering, I am alert to those vanished lives; they move and speak in my mind, and call to one another by name. Most days, however, lacking the mental energy for such awareness, I wander half-asleep through my tasks. Most days, death-forgetting, I feel a touch disoriented, nagged by a suspicion that I've neglected some fundamental obligation whose nature and purpose I cannot name. Late at night, as I lie awake, this oversight assumes outsize dimensions and casts a shadow across the morning's routines.

Crows caw the moon sets frost fills the sky
river maples fishing fires care-plagued sleep
(Chang Chi, "Anchored Overnight at Maple Bridge," 8 CE)[2]

It is with relief and gratitude that I approach age fifty in good health, my faculties intact, not inordinately harassed or embittered, despondent or disillusioned or ill. By historical standards, I am among the most fortunate human beings to have ever been born. The standard of living I've enjoyed throughout my life—running water, a dependable food supply, medical care, immunity to socio-politico-economic injustices—is among the highest ever known.

Having passed the meridian of his life, Erasmus, "content with his mediocrity" and finding in fame no release from the common debt of humanity, decided to devote the remainder of his days to a "meditation about death and the training of my soul," a decision his sixteenth-century contemporaries would consider not morbid but prudent. For all his foresight, however, he died disappointed. But I'll take my warrant from him all the same.

Past the midpoint of this life, my aim is to consult, through books and stories, those who have deeply considered of death. I must assume a listening posture, keep my eyes open and my mouth shut, search for touchstones among those who have met their ends with something like dignity; among those who have pondered, without wavering, their own extinction; and among those who have dwelt in death's proximity long enough to be intimate with it. From all these, I might learn how to face adversity, if not with courage then at least without cowardice; learn how to make of death something more—only a little more—than a gruesome slog.

I want notes from the dungeons: Keats writing as he suffocated, or Akhmatova, tormented with threats of her son's torture and execution, writing nevertheless. Mandelstam survived for years in exile, under threat of execution; the tension ruined his heart, but he did not stop writing poems. His wife Nadezhda, despite the risks, preserved them.

We marvel at the butcher's stall,
the child asleep under a netting of blue flies,
the lamb on the hill, the monk on the ass,
the duke's soldiery, slightly crazed
with wine drinking, plague and garlic,
and more freshly, like the dawn, we marvel at our loss.[3]

Bright despair lives in these lines from a poem titled "Ariosto," written when his arrest was imminent. The lines ring with pity, humor, and forgiveness, and they exude nobility for these reasons. In these lines, I begin to see how compassion, if rendered sincerely, is rendered primarily in the knowledge of death.

When confronted with testimonies like the Mandelstams', the cynicism I often affect amid every modern comfort is a trite indulgence, an affectation borne of fear, the modish pretense of the undeservingly fortunate. My cynicism and my skepticism are profanities. They are gutless, tiresome, and pernicious. They were never very funny.

Greed, pride, war, disease, the pointless waste of life, our ineluctable extinction: these things are given. But there is a choice, I think, that is also given. How will I comport myself on the road to death? Self-regarding, resenting? Or humbly, persevering, ready to the last to grieve with another's loss, to celebrate the small victories of good souls, to keep the example of survivors and of good thieves before my eyes? To be an observant fellow traveler who does not mar the afternoon with complaints, but cheerfully points out to a passerby the halo around the moon. That is who I might be.

"Tell us," the Irish poet asked the Russian one:[4]

Son of Petropolis, tell us,
Tell us how to turn into the flash,
To lie in the lice-red shirt

Figure 1. Paul Cézanne, *The House of the Hanged Man*, 1873, oil on canvas.

On the bank of the Styx and wait
For the gossamer of Paradise
To spider in our dirt-filled eyes.

There is a painting of a house in a village.[5]

The house leans top-heavy, awkwardly situated below the road. When I first saw the painting, I supposed that the chief virtue of the subject, for the painter, lay in the fact that the house faced the setting sun. Perhaps he or she was concerned with the changeable colors of the shadows in a quiet lane, or with a truth revealed in a moment of light on a nameless afternoon.

With these thoughts in mind, I noticed nothing overly remarkable about the house itself, but when I read in the caption the name of the painting, *The House of the Hanged Man*, there was a change. There appeared a darkness behind the two upper windows, misaligned and trimmed with moss. I could not tell if the topmost window was open or missing, or if the place was deserted. The structure of the place seemed to sag for want of warmth and bustle and talk. The house became, essentially and from that time, the hanged man's house.

An awareness of boundaries—the boundary between life and death, present and past—intrudes at times. Workaday commotion subsides, if only briefly, and I'm recalled by the shadow on a brick wall, or the rinsed cup in my hand as I stand at the sink, or a jet's pink contrail on a summer evening.

It's unsettling and unprofitable to dwell on the implications, and there is thankfully no end to the distractions that call me back from these suspicions. The world, ever on guard against such unruly thoughts, soon reimposes its fascinations.

One day, I heard my name spoken in an empty room. The voice was familiar, genial, and it spoke only once. I wonder if this happens to other people. It's not something you bring up very often. There's something almost shameful in it.

Shaxi, Yunnan Province, Southwestern China

The violet water, pocked with little vortices, skims and planes beneath the footbridge, reflecting whorling blue light back on the arch stones. In painting, perspective might be rendered by the simple expedient of diluting the ink. Perspective is a matter of temperature and tone, too, and great skill is called for, to capture these.

Light and water are tricky subjects. Misled by contrasts, I stray into shadings, where I must continually relearn the fact that shadows are colored.

It is hard to make peace with my inability to express even my simplest feelings about light or water, hard to accept that this will always be the case. My lack of understanding is self-evident, yet never ceases to feel, somehow, *unjust*. That's a silly notion, I know.

I'm left with the testimony of my senses, and they're just not reliable.

Even if I were appointed Master of Waters by the Duke of Venice, and spent a lifetime gauging the velocity of rivers, or divining their vectors with a plummet line, I would learn little of water's mysteries. The entirety of my knowledge, after all that, would be as nothing compared to the meanest convict who—chained to his bench below deck, shut away from the sun and the breeze—but once had rowed beyond sight of the coast.

Guangxi Province, Southeast China

A chair was placed in the parcel of sunlight that spilled over the threshold of the open door, and in the chair sat a man. He was old, perhaps eighty, and despite the sultry spring heat, he wore a knit hat and a heavy coat. His head rested deeply in his shoulders.

There is nothing so lonely as illness.

His eyes were open, but not to the sun or to the paper moths that worried the scarred jambs of the entry. One hand was propped on a walking stick, as if he meant to rise to his feet, take the mattock from its hook on the wall, and set off for the terraced gardens below the house, there to dig a few radishes for supper.

A rooster bustled over the threshold and commenced a leisurely search for spiders and stray grains of rice around the man's feet.

Barn swallows darted through the doorway, to and from their mud nests in the rafters. They're welcome to make their homes here. Harbingers of spring, swallows have brought good luck to Chinese homes for millennia. "All summer long village life is peaceful," Tu Fu wrote. "Swallows in the rafters come and go at will."[6]

Four of us—my wife, her mother, her brother, and myself—have come to this house, in a village called Da Jiang ("Big River") in the mountains of Guanxi Province, not far from the border with Vietnam. The place had long been accessible only by boat and footpath, but in recent years an unpaved track has been carved through the forest, just wide enough for a borrowed 4WD Toyota. It was to this village that my wife's mother had been sent, during the Cultural Revolution, to teach mathematics at the village school. Millions of educated city and town dwellers were sent to places like this in those years, in order to acquaint them with the virtues of communal labor. A regimen of work, fresh air, and simple country fare would serve to refine their spirits of the dross of modern life, with its enervating luxuries and toxic ideas.

Hë spent five years at Da Jiang and served the children as best she could. She recalls those years as both difficult and rewarding. I am in most ways a stranger to my wife's family, so there is a limit to what I will learn about her experience. The lack of a shared language is not an obstacle—my wife is happy to translate any questions I have—but Hë will not reveal her deepest feelings on the experience, which involved long separations from home and family. The memory, it is plain, was one that is deeply important to her, and not lightly broached.

When we arrive in the village, we find many of the townsmen gathered on benches in front of a shop to play mahjong. Few of the men are old enough to recall the energetic young teacher who arrived from Guilin fifty years earlier; no one recognizes her, but they all know where the old school principal lives. We shoulder our packs for a short hike through a bamboo grove, down a path of mud-slick stones, to the rambling farmhouse overlooking the reservoir.

Ten years have passed since her last visit, and in that time the principal's health has deteriorated. His son served as principal, too, has retired in his turn, and now cares for his father. The younger man greets us at the gate, and we stow our gear and gather in the kitchen for lunch.

The principal's son has been busy cooking fish, gathering and cutting greens and mushrooms, digging roots, washing dishes. These duties are in addition to the everyday tasks of cultivating cedar trees, beekeeping, tending the chickens, and caring for the old man. All day long he hurries about in gumboots, shouldering a carrying pole or a mattock from tomato garden to chicken coop, from town to lake. He prepares three meals a day, with help today from the visitors. At mealtimes, we perch on short stools in a capacious and ill-lit kitchen of smoke-blackened walls, eating boiled greens and fish and rice, spitting the bones on the floor for the kittens, cats, and chickens that pace restively beneath the table.

paper ashes fly like snow-white butterflies
tears from broken hearts stain azaleas red
foxes sleep in tombs once the sun goes down
(Kao Chu, "Drinking Wine on Grave Sweeping Day," 12 CE)[7]

Hë pulls a chair up beside the old man and speaks cheerfully to him as she massages his neck and shoulders, scalp and ears. He rallies now and then with a word or a laugh, but mostly he submits quietly to her care.

In the afternoon we climb the path behind the farmhouse, through the blank and muggy air, to the cemetery set into the hillside. After a brief search, the principal's son and Hë find the tomb belonging to a man they refer to as "the widower." During her long sojourn here, Hë befriended this widower, swept his rooms, and fetched water for him daily from the well. When he died, there was no one to tend his grave, or to burn incense during the festival of the dead, or to clear the brush that rapidly overtakes the tombs in this semitropical place. These tasks, therefore, are the business of the hour, for today is Chingming, Grave Sweeping Day.

Just above and behind the widower's tomb, to right and left—set like eyes, as it were, relative to the tomb's mouth—are two smaller tombs that belong to the male and female guardian spirits. These, too, must be cleared and purified with smoke, so that they might perform their duties more efficiently. There is no ritual silence to all this work, no self-conscious lowering of voices, just a glad and unhurried tidying.

When all is in order again, we return to the house where we sit overlooking the reservoir. The mountains beyond the water are cloaked in mist. A pair of coucals—vivid bronze and black, thirty inches long from head to tail—make regular flights back and forth across the little valley below, between their hidden home and a bamboo grove. They are plainly visible from our vantage point as they stalk the undergrowth for grubs.

Now and then, the disembodied sound of a boat motor weaves through the chorus of insects.

As we sit in the hazy heat, Hë tells her children about her experiences as a young teacher. Mornings, she said, she used to ferry her pupils across the river in her arms, so they could arrive dry-shod at school. This duty was performed year-round, in winter and high water. She speaks of the separation from her family and loved ones during those years, and falls silent for a time.

In keeping with a custom I don't fully understand, she has been asked by the old principal to join his family. This is not an honorific or a courtesy or a gesture of affection; it involves real and often onerous responsibilities, such as tending his grave when he dies. A similar request in the past, I've learned, had been denied. She deliberates a few days on the matter. The trip from her home to this place is long, jolting, and not served by bus. And she is no longer young.

In the end, she assents to the old man's request. On the morning we are to depart, she massages his neck and speaks smilingly to him of many things, and we leave him seated in the chair, in the slanting light, a blanket spread neatly across his knees.

Gansu Province, Western China

At the southern edge of the Gobi Desert, north of the Qilian Mountains, the Dachuan River flows beneath a sheer sandstone cliff. According to legend, a monk named Le Zun arrived here sometime in the fourth century and experienced a vision of a thousand Buddhas. Over the next millennium, Le Zun's cave expanded into a complex of hundreds of grottoes, and the place became known as Qianfodong, Caves of a Thousand Buddhas, or more simply as the Mogao Caves. The grottoes are covered with murals depicting episodes from the life of the Buddha, and images of paradise, too: pipa players and demonesses, famous disciples and guardian warriors, archers on horseback and Immortals on mountaintops.

Mogao became an important stop on the Silk Road. In those days, ideas traveled virally, carried by armies and caravans back and forth across Asia, infecting nations along the way with new philosophies and new religions. For centuries, followers of Islam and Christianity—merchants and pilgrims—paused at Mogao to replenish their supplies, and to marvel at the stone Buddha rising one hundred feet to the apex of a cave.

There are traces on these walls of that long-ago, east-west cross-pollination. Some of the guardian warriors who flank the Buddha wear bushy red beards; their blue eyes and fleshy faces recall characters from a Dostoevsky novel. Buddha seated on a throne resembles a Byzantine Christ, a folded white robe draped over one shoulder, his right hand raised in a gesture meant, as I understand, to dispel fear or to instill calm.

It was a visionary age. Four thousand miles to the west of here, near the time when the monk Le Zun experienced his visions in these caves, a young man gave his inheritance to the poor and made his way into the desert. Anthony, like Le Zun, prized solitude, and "loved more than all things his sojourn in the mountain," in the wilderness of Lower Egypt.[8] There, according to Athanasius's *Life*, he found that place of still waters, known to the Desert Fathers and Mothers as the "inner mountain," a place accessible solely to the brokenhearted.

Both Le Zun and Anthony attracted visitors and disciples, men and women who made difficult and dangerous journeys to the wilderness to share in the monks' visions, to study their discipline, to ponder transience or to lose themselves in it.

Artisans from Mongolia, India, and central Asia came to Mogao to paint murals and carve statues. Wealthy merchants funded the work, and the donors' images remain vivid in detail and color. Their expressions are serenely pious, satisfied in the foreknowledge that they had, in some small measure, cheated death.

The merchants, however, eventually found sea routes that lay beyond the reach of desert marauders, the Silk Road changed course, and by the time the last Crusades were grinding to a close, the caves at Mogao had been abandoned to shepherds and nomads and solitary monks. In the nineteenth and early twentieth centuries, Western Orientalists came to excavate the caves and carry off statues and scrolls. The cave's interiors today are scarred by the crude efforts of Americans and Europeans to remove the ancient murals. In the course of this long theft, much was destroyed. Other caves were damaged by soldiers during the wars and revolutions that have swept across China over the last hundred years.

And the Dachuan slowly dried up.

At the end of the Second World War, a young woman arrived at Mogao as part of a small contingent of artists and scholars commissioned by the revolutionary government to study and preserve the murals. A photo of Li Qiqong, taken during the early years of the Republic, shows a small figure in a Red Army tunic and cap. A young woman, clear-eyed and curious; self-conscious in the manner of young soldiers, but not without a touch of amusement about it. The formal pose and uniform cannot entirely conceal a native generosity in her expression.

From that time until the end of her life, except for brief periods of political exile, Li worked to reproduce, on paper and with painstaking exactitude, the murals at Mogao.

A collection of her work was on display, at the time of our visit, at the exhibition center at Mogao. The center was deserted, and her pictures hung in twilit silence. Here were Immortals frozen in dervish dances, and holy ascetics beset by demons and lurking dragons. Trailing long silken wings, the flying apsaras—female wind spirits, some with black faces—troubled the banyan trees.

Li was especially drawn to the many depictions of flora and fauna in the grottoes: hummingbirds; deer abounding; a bodhisattva carrying flowers in a glass; and the Buddha, in one of his myriad incarnations, offering the flesh of his body to nourish a starving tigress and her cubs.

As an altar boy in Cincinnati, holding the paten for the priest during the Eucharist, I had little idea what the ritual signified, and I often stared impolitely as the parishioners filed up in their hundreds, hands folded, to take the wafer on their tongue.

Body of Christ. Amen. Body of Christ. Amen. Body of Christ.

Thirty-five years later, looking at Li's rendition of the young prince kneeling before the hungry cubs, I find a new light shed on an old difficulty. The persistence of such mysteries presents a reminder of the need, old as humanity, to find meaning in death. To undertake this old dark search is to participate in a tradition that binds me, however tenuously, to Li, to Anthony, and to everyone who has ever lived long enough to open their eyes. There is meaning in this search, despite, and perhaps because of, its hopelessness. Sometimes, Li once told an interviewer, when she was engrossed in her labors in a candlelit cave, alone and not alone among the nameless vanished artists, she emerged from a night of work to find wolf prints in the sand at the cave's mouth.

Her devotion to history, both Chinese and Buddhist, attracted the hostility and suspicion of the powers that be, and she was twice denounced as a reactionary. Flying apsaras and starving tigresses were not welcome during the Great Leap Forward or the Cultural Revolution. Like Le Zun and Anthony in Lower Egypt, Li Qiqong was a death-remembering woman in a death-forgetting world. The world, needless to say, is not friendly to such ones. Nevertheless, she outlived them and continued well into her nineties to paint and study and teach.[9]

Dunhuang, Gansu Province

The temple courtyard is deserted. The bells, steles, and broken cauldrons arrayed about the place are transfixed by the midday sun, meticulously abandoned to the heat.

Barn swallows rifle through the temple doors. Inside the temple, above the statue of Buddha, the birds look down from their mud nests, calmly regarding the intruders. With their dark gorgets and slender black wings clasped at the tail, they resemble underfed clerks at a medieval abbey.

I'm given to moody silences and useless brooding. "We're very lucky," my wife says, reading my thoughts again. "There's a lot of unhappiness in the world." The flat fact of her statement strikes me as superfluous and startling, like a reminder to breathe. She knows how I get.

But I think the silence of the temple grounds has set her wondering as well. There's a wakefulness to deserted places, like this temple. A restiveness not unlike thought.

A series of murals on the temple courtyard wall relates how a young man left his father's house and went out into the world, there to suffer at the sight of pain. And here again, as at the nearby Mogao caves, I find an image of a prince kneeling before a litter of hungry tiger cubs.

That there is a mutual dependence between the living and the dead, between destruction and creation, is no new idea, but one that belongs to the oldest stories. And those stories are the bread that nourishes the living and the dead, else remembrance were nonsense, and posterity sheer delirium.

In another painting in the courtyard is the figure of a young man seated cross-legged on the earth. Around his head is a nimbus of flames like the gold-leaf halo worn by one of Fra Angelico's Madonnas.

In the symbology of this art, fire recalls the pain of desire, or the pain of ignorance. Perhaps both are intended. Flowers drift around the figure like the notes of a celestial music, and the figure's eyes are closed in rapture to the melody.

We wander the grounds, past a pair of groundskeepers resting on a bench beside their outsize brush brooms. In a corner of the temple grounds, in the shade of apricot trees, a hoopoe is feeding, displaying the fan of a crest as it probes the dry earth with its bill.

Beyond the courtyard walls, the Singing Sands tower hundreds of feet in the air. The curved, clean lines of the dunes waver as in a fever.

notes

King Oedipus

1. Sophocles, *Oedipus at Colonus*, 144.
2. Euripides. *Alcestis*, 44.
3. Underhill, *Ruysbroeck*, 171.
4. Sophocles, *Oedipus at Colonus*, 174.

Light Discipline

1. Ward, *The Desert Fathers*, 24.
2. Acts 26:24, King James Version (henceforth KJV).

The Cloud of Unknowing

1. Copleston, *A History of Philosophy*, Part I: Pre-Mediaeval Influences, chapter 2, "The Patristic Period."
2. Wolters, *The Cloud of Unknowing*, chapter XXXII.
3. Wolters, *The Cloud of Unknowing*, chapters XIII and XIV.
4. Wolters, *The Cloud of Unknowing*, chapter XLIII.
5. Gallacher, *The Cloud of Unknowing*.
6. Wolters, *The Cloud of Unknowing*, chapter VIII.
7. Wolters, *The Cloud of Unknowing*, chapter XXIV.
8. Wolters, *The Cloud of Unknowing*, chapter III.
9. Gallacher, *The Cloud of Unknowing*.
10. Underhill, *A Book of Contemplation*, chapter XXXV.
11. Gallacher, *The Cloud of Unknowing*.

Hell on Ducks

1. Huizinga, *Erasmus*, 22.
2. Sir Thomas Browne, *Religio Medici*, part I.

3. Inge, *The Philosophy of Plotinus.*

4. Jones, *Studies in Mystical Religion*, chapter IV.

5. Mirandola, *Oration on the Dignity of Man.*

6. Huizinga, *Erasmus and the Age of Reformation*, chapter XII.

7. Huizinga, *Erasmus and the Age of Reformation*, Letter IV, "To James Batt," Orléans [c. 12 December] 1500.

8. Huizinga, *Erasmus and the Age of Reformation*, Letter XIII "To Beatus Rhenanus," Louvain [c. 15 October] 1518.

9. Huizinga, *Erasmus and the Age of Reformation*, Letter XI, "To Wolfgang Fabricius Capito," Antwerp, 26 February 1516/17.

10. Huizinga, *Erasmus and the Age of Reformation*. Letter XIV, "To Martin Luther," Louvain, 30 May 1519.

11. Huizinga, *Erasmus and the Age of Reformation*, chapter XIII.

12. Huizinga, *Erasmus and the Age of Reformation*, chapter XXI.

13. Huizinga, *Erasmus and the Age of Reformation*, chapter XX.

14. Huizinga, *Erasmus and the Age of Reformation*, chapter XX.

15. Psalm 14, KJV.

16. Becker, *The Heavenly City.*

A Brief History of the Huron

1. Barzun, *Dawn to Decadence.*

2. Parkman, *The Jesuits in North America*, chapter II.

3. Parkman, *The Jesuits in North America*, chapter XXII.

4. Parkman, *The Jesuits in North America*, chapter V.

5. Parkman, *The Jesuits in North America*, "Introduction."

6. Parkman, *The Jesuits in North America*, chapter X.

7. Parkman, *The Jesuits in North America*, chapter XIII.

8. Parkman, *The Jesuits in North America*, chapter VIII.

9. Parkman, *The Jesuits in North America*, chapter XI.

10. Parkman, *The Jesuits in North America*, chapter XV.

11. Parkman, *The Jesuits in North America*, chapter IX.

12. Blunden, *Undertones of War*, 20.

13. Ezekiel 37, KJV.

14. Le Goff, *Saint Francis of Assisi*, 103.

Winter in the Capital

1. Revelation 21:1, KJV.

2. See Jones, *Studies in Mystical Religion*, chapter XX, 495.

3. Fox, *An Autobiography*, chapter VII, 196.

4. Wordsworth, "Prospectus," 445, lines 47–51. The "Prospectus" was taken from *Home at Grasmere* to form the conclusion to *The first Book of the Recluse*, which was never published.

5. Wordsworth, *The Prelude*, Book XIII, 369, lines 128–29.

6. Dorothy Wordsworth, *The Grasmere and Alfoxden Journals.*

7. Wordsworth, *The Prelude*, Book VII, 274–75, lines 626–36.

8. Keats, "Letter to John Hamilton Reynolds," 108.

9. à Kempis, *His Age and Book*, 269.

10. Wordsworth, "Mutability," *Ecclesiastical Sonnets*, Part III. XXXIV, 449.

Spring Arrives in the Gobi

1. Dorothy Wordsworth, *Grasmere and Alfoxden Journals*, April 20, 1801, p. 88.

2. Virgil, *Georgics,* Book II.

3. Brazil, *Birds of East Asia.*

4. Sara Coleridge, *Memoir and Letters of Sara Coleridge*, Letter IX ("To the Same," October 4, 1837), 148.

5. Silvestris, *The Cosmographia*, 109.

6. Ovid, *Metamorphoses*, Book I, "Chaos and Creation," 4.

7. Virgil, *Aeneid*, Book I, lines 77–84.

8. Cusa, "On Learned Ignorance."

9. Boas, *Primitivism and Related Ideas*, 173.

10. Ovid, *Metamorphoses*, Book IX.

11. Milton, *Paradise Regained*, Book IV, 310.

12. Nordhoff and Hall, *Men Against the Sea.*

A Natural History of New Mexico

1. MacCaig, "The Sinai Sort."

2. "Luís de Velasco, 1597," 429–33.

3. Russel, *The History of Mexico*, 101.

4. Knaut, *The Pueblo Revolt*, 129.

5. "New Mexico, 1629–1671," 139–40. With gratitude to Mr. Andrew L. Knaut, and to his book, for drawing the reader's attention to the potent symbolism in the extraordinary transformation that occurred between the departure of de Velasco and the return, decades later, of de Aguilar.

6. Knaut, *The Pueblo Revolt*, 138.

7. Erdoes and Ortiz, "Creation of First Man and First Woman," 39.

8. Momaday, *Man Made of Words*, 85.

9. Adamson, *American Indian Literature.*

10. Erdoes and Ortiz, "Creation of First Man and First Woman," 40.

11. Genesis 1:2, KJV.

12. Psalm 135:7, KJV.

13. Tyndale, *New Testament of 1526*, "The Gospell of S. Jhon," iii.

14. Berdyaev, *Destiny of Man*, 141.

The Rock Cycle

1. Da Vinci, *Notebooks*, Part II. The Universe, (a), "The Deluge and Shells," 27.

2. Da Vinci, *Notebooks*, Part II. The Universe, (a), "The Deluge and Shells," 35.

3. Hutton, *Theory of the Earth*, volume I, part I, chapter I, section IV.

4. Hutton, "Abstract," from his dissertation titled *Concerning the System of the Earth, its Duration and Stability*, presented to the Royal Society on July 4, 1785. This abstract was circulated privately. The completed work appeared in 1788 as *Theory of the Earth, or an Investigation of the Laws observable in the Composition, Dissolution, and Restoration of Land upon the Globe.*

5. Hutton, "Abstract."

6. Eiseley, "How the World Became Natural," 148.

7. Hutton, "Abstract."

8. Eiseley, "How the World Became Natural," 148.

9. Ovid, *Metamorphoses*, 430.

10. Strabo, quoted in Steno, *Prodromus*, 210.

11. Nicolson, *Mountain Gloom and Mountain Glory*, 148

12. White, *A History of the Warfare of Science with Theology*, 214.

13. The name for the chemical element Ni and the five-cent coin comes from the German *kupfernickel*, a mischievous, mine-dwelling gnome.

14. Burton, *Anatomy of Melancholy*, The Second Partition, Section 2: "Diet, etc., Rectified; with a Digression of Air," 21.

15. Hutton, *Theory of the Earth*, volume II, chapter VIII.

16. Baxter, *Ages in Chaos*, 212.

17. Pithawalla, *An Introduction to Kashmir*, 11.

18. *Geneva Bible of 1560*, Genesis, chapter VI.

19. Milton, *Paradise Lost*, Book IX, lines 783–84.

20. This version of the story of Cain and Abel is found in *Geneva Bible of 1560*, Genesis, chapter IV.2.

21. *Geneva Bible of 1560*, chapter IV.9.

22. Nicolson, *Mountain Gloom*, 71.

23. *Geneva Bible of 1560*, chapter IV.10–11.

24. Nicolson, *Mountain Gloom*, 71.

25. Nicolson, *Mountain Gloom*, 102.

26. *Imperial Gazetteer of India*, volume XV, "Karachi to Kotayam," 73.

27. Collier, *Cosmogonies*, 444.

28. Butterfield, *The Origins of Modern Science*, 235.

29. Collier, *Cosmogonies*, 429.

30. Eiseley, *Night Country*, 144.

31. Koestler, *The Sleepwalkers*, "Preface," 11.

32. Job 38:4, KJV.

33. Voltaire is here paraphrased in Miller, *Testimony of the Rocks*, "Lecture Eighth: The Noachian Deluge," 279.

34. Goethe's criticisms of Voltaire are presented in Miller, *Testimony of the Rocks*, 323.

35. Steno, *Prodromus*, 215.

36. Cutler, *The Seashell on the Mountaintop*, 38.

37. Cutler, *Seashell*, 123.

38. Steno, *Prodromus*, 263.

39. O'Carroll, "Nicolas Steno."

40. Jefferson, "Species Extinction."

41. Eiseley, "How Death Became Natural," 156.

42. Nicolson, *Mountain Gloom*, 156.

43. Cutler, *The Seashell on the Mountaintop*.

44. Cutler, *The Seashell on the Mountaintop*.

45. Cutler, *The Seashell on the Mountaintop*.

46. Cioni, *Niels Stensen*, 185.

Verdun

1. Horne, *The Price of Glory*, 326. This observation appeared in the Reichsarchiv, the official German postwar account of the war's major battles.

2. Horne, *The Price of Glory*, 118.

3. Horne, *The Price of Glory*, 176.

4. Horne, *The Price of Glory*, 198.

Cycling the Mojave

1. van Dyke, *The Desert*, 107.

2. van Dyke, *The Desert*, 93.

3. Conron, *The American Landscape*, 351. Powell's account first appeared in 1895 as *The Exploration of the Colorado River and its Canyons*.

4. O'Donnell, *Augustine: Confessions*, volume II, *Commentary* on Books 1–7, page 140.

5. Williams, *Wilderness and Paradise*, 13.

6. Jones, *Spiritual Reformers*.

The Western Terminus

1. Red Pine, *Poems of the Masters*, 2003. Note pertains to his translation of Tu Fu's "Miscellaneous Poem at Chinchou," 166.

2. Red Pine, *Poems of the Masters*, "Anchored Overnight at Maple Bridge" by Chang Chi, 195.

3. Mandel'shtam, *Selected Poems*, "Ariosto," 125.

4. Deane, *Selected Poems*, "Osip Mandelstam," 39.

5. Paul Cézanne, *The House of the Hanged Man*, 1873, oil on canvas.

6. Red Pine, *Poems of the Masters*, 411.

7. Red Pine, *Poems of the Masters*, "Drinking Wine on Grave Sweeping Day" by Kao Chu, 395.

8. Athanasius, *Select Writings*.

9. Information in English regarding the Chinese artist Li Qiqong is difficult to find. This information is taken from personal notes of our brief visit, and from memory, and is therefore not as reliable as I would wish.

works cited

Adamson, Joni. *American Indian Literature, Environmental Justice, and Ecocriticism.* Tucson: The University of Arizona Press, 2001.

à Kempis, Thomas. *His Age and Book.* Edited by J. E. G. de Montmorency. New York: G. P. Putnam's Sons, 1906.

Athanasius, *Life of Anthony.* Translated by Philip Schaff and Henry Wace. *A Select Library of Nicene and Post-Nicene Fathers of the Christian Church,* Vol. IV, Saint Athanasius Select Works and Letters. New York: The Christian Literature Company, 1892.

Barzun, Jacques. *From Dawn to Decadence: 500 Years of Western Cultural Life.* New York: HarperCollins, 2000.

Baxter, Stephen. *Ages in Chaos: James Hutton and the Discovery of Deep Time.* New York: Forge, 2003.

Becker, Carl. *The Heavenly City of the Eighteenth-Century Philosophers.* New Haven: Yale University Press, 1932.

Berdyaev, Nicolas. *The Destiny of Man.* Translated by Natalie Duddington. London: G. Bles, 1937.

Blunden, Edmund. *Undertones of War.* University of Chicago Press, 2007.

Boas, George. *Primitivism and Related Ideas in the Middle Ages.* Baltimore: The Johns Hopkins University Press, 1997.

Brazil, Mark. *Birds of East Asia.* Princeton Field Guides. Princeton University Press, 2009.

Browne, Sir Thomas. *Religion Medici. The Major Works.* Edited by C. A. Patrides. New York: Penguin Classics, 1977.

Burton, Robert. *The Anatomy of Melancholy.* New York Review of Books, 2001.

Butterfield, Herbert. *The Origins of Modern Science.* London: The Free Press, 1957.

Cioni, Raffaello. *Niels Stensen: Scientist-Bishop.* New York: P. J. Kennedy and Sones, 1962.

Coleridge, Sara. *Memoir and Letters of Sara Coleridge,* New York: Harper and Brothers, 1874.

Collier, Katherine Brownell. *Cosmogonies of Our Fathers: Some Theories of the 17. and the 18. Centuries*. London: Octagon, 1968.
Conron, John. *The American Landscape: A Critical Anthology of Prose and Poetry*. Oxford University Press, 1973.
Copleston, S. J. Frederick. *A History of Philosophy*, Volume II: Augustine to Scotus. Paulist Press, 1950.
Erdoes, Richard, and Alfonso Ortiz. "Creation of First Man and First Woman." In *American Indian Myths and Legends*, edited by Richard Erdoes and Alfonso Ortiz, 39. Pantheon Books, 1984.
Cusa, Nicholas. "On Learned Ignorance." In *Renaissance Philosophy*, Vol. II: The Transalpine Thinkers, 75. New York: The Modern Library, 1969.
Cutler, Alan. *The Seashell on the Mountaintop*. New York: Dutton, 2003.
Da Vinci, Leonardo. *Notebooks*. Edited by Irma A. Richter. Oxford University Press, 2008.
Deane, Seamus. *Selected Poems*. Oldcastle, Ireland: The Gallery Press, 1988.
Eiseley, Loren. "How the World Became Natural." In *The Firmament of Time. Collected Essays on Evolution, Nature, and the Cosmos*, edited by William Cronon, 148. Boone, IA: Library of America, 2016.

———. "How Death Became Natural." In *The Firmament of Time. Collected Essays on Evolution, Nature, and the Cosmos*, edited by William Cronon, 156. Boone, IA: The Library of America, 2016.
———. *Night Country*. Lincoln: University of Nebraska Press, 1997.
Euripides, *The Bacchae*. Translated by William Arrowsmith. *Greek Tragedies III*, edited by Mark Griffith, David Grene, & Richmond Lattimore. University of Chicago Press, 2013.
———. *Alcestis*. Translated by Richard Lattimore. *Greek Tragedies III*, edited by Mark Griffith, David Grene, & Richmond Lattimore. University of Chicago Press, 2013.
Fox, George. *An Autobiography*, edited by Rufus M. Jones. Philadelphia: Ferris and Leach, 1909.
Gallacher, Patrick J, ed. *The Cloud of Unknowing*. TEAMS: Middle English Texts Series, The University of Rochester, 1997. https://d.lib.rochester.edu/teams/text/gallacher-cloud-of-unknowing.
Geneva Bible of 1560 [Facsimile of the 1560 Edition]. Peabody, MA: Hendrickson Publishers, 2007.
Horne, Alistair. *The Price of Glory: Verdun 1916*. New York: Penguin, 1993.
Huizinga, Johan. *Erasmus*. Translated by F. Hopman. New York: Charles Scribner's & Sons, 1924.
———. *Erasmus and the Age of Reformation: with a Selection of the Letters of Erasmus*. Translated by F. Hopman and Barbara Flower. New York: Harper & Row, 1957.

Hutton, James. "Abstract," *Concerning the System of the Earth, its Duration and Stability*. http://pages.uwc.edu/keith.montgomery/Hutton/Abstract-facsimile/abstract1.htm. Accessed March 1, 2020.

———. *Theory of the Earth*. Volume I. The Project Gutenberg, July 2004. http://www.gutenberg.org/files/12861/12861-h/12861-h.htm. Accessed January 15, 2020.

———. *Theory of the Earth*. Volume II. The Project Gutenberg, July 2004. http://www.gutenberg.org/files/14179/14179-h/14179-h.htm. Accessed January 15, 2020.

Inge, William Ralph. *The Philosophy of Plotinus: The Gifford Lectures at St. Andrews, 1917–1918*. London: Longmans, Green and Co., 1918.

Jefferson, Thomas. "Species Extinction: Notes on the State of Virginia." *The Jefferson Monticello*. https://www.monticello.org/site/research-and-collections/species-extinction. Accessed March 1 2020.

Jones, Rufus, M. *Spiritual Reformers in the 16th and 17th Centuries*. New York: Macmillan, 1914.

———. *Studies in Mystical Religion*. London: Macmillan and Co., Ltd., 1919.

Keats, John. "Letter to John Hamilton Reynolds." In *Letters of John Keats*, edited by Sidney Colvin, 108. London, Macmillan and Co., 1891.

Knaut, Andrew L. *The Pueblo Revolt of 1680: Conquest and Resistance in Seventeenth-Century New Mexico*. Norman: University of Oklahoma Press, 1997.

Koestler, Arthur. *The Sleepwalkers: A History of Man's Changing Vision of the Universe*. New York: Penguin, 1986.

Le Goff, Jacques. *Saint Francis of Assisi*. Translated by Christine Rhone. London: Routledge, 1999.

Lopez, Barry. *Crossing Open Ground*. New York: Vintage, 1989.

"Luís de Velasco, 1597." In *Historical Documents Relating to New Mexico, Nueva Vizcaya, and Approaches Thereto, to 1773*, vol. 1, edited by Charles Wilson Hackett, 429–33. Washington, DC: Carnegie Institution of Washington, 1923.

MacCaig, Norman. "The Sinai Sort." In *The Sinai Sort*. London: Hogarth Press, 1957.

Mandel'shtam, Osip. *Selected Poems*. London: Writers and Readers, 1983.

Miller, Hugh. *The Testimony of the Rocks: Geology in Its Bearing on the Two Theologies, Natural and Revealed*. Edinburgh, 1857.

Miller, J. Hillis. *The Disappearance of God: Five Nineteenth-Century Writers*. Cambridge, MA: Harvard University Press, 1963.

Milton, John. *Paradise Lost*. Oxford University Press, 2005.

———. *Paradise Regained, Samson Agonistes, and the Complete Shorter Poems*, edited by William Kerrigan, John Rumrich, and Stephen M. Fallon. New York: The Modern Library, 2012.

Mirandola, della, Giovanni Pico. *Oration on the Dignity of Man*. Vancouver, Canada: Anvil Press, 1953.

Momaday, N. Scott. *Man Made of Words*. New York: St. Martin's Press, 1997.

"New Mexico, 1629–1671." *Historical Documents Relating to New Mexico, Nueva Vizcaya, and Approaches Thereto, to 1773*, vol. 3, edited by Charles Wilson Hackett, 139–40. Washington, DC: Carnegie Institution of Washington, 1937.

Nicolson, Marjorie Hope. *Mountain Gloom and Mountain Glory: The Development of the Aesthetics of the Infinite*. Seattle: University of Washington Press, 1997.

Nordhoff, Charles, and James Hall. *Men Against the Sea*. New York: Little, Brown, and Company, 1964.

O'Carroll, Eoin. "Nicolas Steno: The saint who undermined creationism." *The Christian Science Monitor*, 11 Jan. 2012, https://www.csmonitor.com/Technology/Horizons/2012/0111/Nicolas-Steno-The-saint-who-undermined-creationism. Accessed 15 Sept. 2016.

O'Donnell, James Joseph. *Augustine*: *Confessions*, Vol. II, *Commentary* on Books 1–7. Oxford University Press, 2012.

Ovid, *Metamorphoses*. Translated by Horace Gregory. Signet Classics, 2009.

Parkman, Francis. *The Jesuits in North America in the Seventeenth Century*. 1867. Boone, IA: Library of America, 1983.

———. *Pioneers of France in the New World*. 1865. Boone, IA: Library of America, 1983.

Pithawalla, Maneck B. *An Introduction to Kashmir: Its Geology and Geography*. Kashmir Publications, 1953.

Red Pine. *Poems of the Masters: China's Classic Anthology of T'ang and Sung Dynasty Verse*. Port Townsend, WA: Copper Canyon Press, 2003.

Russell, Philip. *The History of Mexico: From Pre-Conquest to Present*. New York: Routledge, 2011.

Silvestris, Bernardus. *The Cosmographia*. Translated by Winthrop Wetherbee. New York: Columbia University Press, 1990.

Sophocles. *Oedipus at Colonus*. Translated by Robert Fitzgerald. *Greek Tragedies III*, edited by Mark Griffith, David Grene, & Richmond Lattimore. University of Chicago Press, 2013.

Steno Nicolaus. *The Prodromus of Nicolaus Steno's Dissertation Concerning a Solid Body Enclosed by Process of Nature Within a Solid*. Translated by John Garrett Winter. New York: Macmillan, 1916.

Sutherland Cotton, James, Richard Burn, and William Stevenson Meyer, eds. *Imperial Gazetteer of India*. Oxford: Clarendon Press, 1908.

Tyndale, William, trans. *The New Testament 1526*, edited by W. R. Cooper. London: The British Library, 2000.

Underhill, Evelyn, trans. and ed. *A Book of Contemplation: The which is Called The Cloud of Unknowing, in the which a Soul is Oned with God.* London: J. M. Watkins, 1922.

———. *Ruysbroeck.* Cosimo, Inc., 2007.

van Dyke, John Charles. *The Desert: Further Studies in Natural Appearances.* London: Charles Scribner's Sons, 1922.

Virgil. *Aeneid.* Translated by Robert Fitzgerald. New York: Vintage Books, 1990.

———. *Georgics.* Translated by C. Day Lewis. Oxford University Press, 1983.

Ward, Benedicta, translator and editor. *The Desert Fathers: Sayings of the Early Christian Monks.* New York: Penguin, 2003.

White, Andrew D. *A History of the Warfare of Science with Theology in Christendom.* London: Macmillan, 1896.

Williams, George H. *Wilderness and Paradise in Christian Thought: The Biblical Experience of the Desert in the History of Christianity & the Paradise Theme in the Theological Idea of the University.* Eugene, OR: Wipf and Stock Publishers, 1962.

Wolters, Clifton, trans. *The Cloud of Unknowing.* New York: Penguin, 1961.

Wordsworth, William. "Mutability." *Ecclesiastical Sonnets,* Part III, xxxiv, *The Collected Poems of William Wordsworth.* Hertfordshire: Wordsworth Editions Limited, 1994.

———. *Prelude, The. Wordsworth's Poetry and Prose.* Edited by Nicholas Halmi. New York: W. W. Norton & Co., 2014.

———. "Prospectus." *The. Wordsworth's Poetry and Prose.* Edited by Nicholas Halmi. New York: W. W. Norton & Co., 2014.

Wordsworth, Dorothy. *The Grasmere and Alfoxden Journals.* Edited by Pamela Woof. Oxford University Press, 2002.

Wright, James A. "In Response to a Rumor That the Oldest Whorehouse in Wheeling, West Virginia Has Been Condemned." In *Above the River: The Complete Poems,* edited by Anne Wright, 173. Middletown, CT: Wesleyan University Press, 1990.